GREAT RECKONINGS
IN LITTLE ROOMS

Bert O. States

Great Reckonings in Little Rooms

On the Phenomenology of Theater

University of California Press

Berkeley   Los Angeles   London

University of California Press
Berkeley and Los Angeles, California
University of California Press, Ltd.
London, England
©1985 by
The Regents of the University of California Press
Printed in the United States of America

1   2   3   4   5   6   7   8   9

First Paperback Printing 1987

**LIBRARY OF CONGRESS CATALOGING
IN PUBLICATION DATA**

States, Bert O., 1929–
  Great reckonings in little rooms.
  Includes index.
  1. Theater. 2. Semiotics. 3. Acting. I. Title.
II. Title: Phenomenology of theater.
PN2041.S45S73   1985   792   84–8616
ISBN 0-520-06182-9

To
KENNETH BURKE

Contents

Acknowledgments

Parts of this book have been published earlier. Chapter 1 is reprinted, with slight revisions, from "The Dog on the Stage: Theater as Phenomenon," in *New Literary History* (Winter 1983). Sections of chapters 4 and 5 appeared first in *Hudson Review* (Autumn 1981) as "Phenomenology of the Curtain Call," and in *Theatre Journal* (October 1983) as "The Actor's Presence: Three Phenomenal Modes." Several paragraphs in chapter 5 are taken from my essay, "Horatio—Our Man in Elsinore: An Essay on Dramatic Logic," in *South Atlantic Quarterly* (Winter 1979). Finally, certain material in the Introduction is taken from my review of Patrice Pavis's *Languages of the Stage* in *Theatre Survey* (May 1984). I am grateful to the editors for permission to republish here.

Among my friends and colleagues, I especially want to thank Paul Hernadi and Mark Rose, of the University of California at Santa Barbara, for their careful and patient readings of the manuscript before it had decided what it wanted to be. Also, John Harrop, of my own department, for our many conversations on acting and actors. Finally, I must mention my good fortune in having a virtually ideal reader for the Press in James L. Calderwood, of the University of California at Irvine.

We were given the power to create
water and earth, air and light on
our stage and to form people after
our own image. . . . Here on our
stage you have wept without
misery, been happy without
cause, gracious without purpose
and unhappy with an inner
happiness, deeply moving
yourself and others to tears—
and all for nothing, for Hecuba.

—*Max Reinhardt*

Introduction

This is a book about the theater phenomenon. It is an extension of notes on the theater and theatergoing that have been accumulating for some time. It does not have an argument, or set out to prove a thesis, and it will not be one of those useful books one reads for the fruits of its research. Moreover, it is not even a phenomenology of the theater, properly speaking. Such a project, as I understand it, would imply a far more thorough and scientific consideration of every aspect of theater than I have presented here. Rather, I have tried to write a form of critical description that is phenomenological in the sense that it focuses on the activity of theater *making itself* out of its essential materials: speech, sound, movement, scenery, text, etc. Like most phenomenological description, it will succeed to the extent that it awakens the reader's memory of his own perceptual encounters with theater. If the book fails in this I imagine it will be about as interesting to read as an anthology of someone else's dreams. In any case, I am less concerned with the scientific purity of my perspective and method than with retrieving something from the theater experience that seems to me worthy of our critical admiration.

We may come closer to the nature of this "something" by posing an old question to which there is surely no adequate answer: What is the origin of theater? A historical explanation would probably refer us to the ritual function of securing various advantages for the community. A phenomenological explanation would begin by asking the question in another way: What kind of being would choose impersonation as a means of securing *any* advantage? Surely theater's origins and purposes are not exhausted in the idea that man wants to imitate the world, as it is or as it should be, or to make the crops do his bidding, or to honor the gods, or simply to entertain his fellow man, if by that we mean offering fictions about his social and private life. If impersonation has the power to do these things, then the power itself must be prior to and independent of them. For the work of art, Heidegger says, is characterized by the fact that it is never "used up"; it does not, like the tool, "disappear into usefulness."[1] It remains beneath all purposes an assertion of a certain power to create, to bring forth. What is it that is brought forth? We find this helpful beginning in Heidegger's essay on the origin of the work of art:

[The sculpture] is not a portrait whose purpose is to make it easier to realize how the god looks; rather, it is a work that lets the god himself be present and thus *is* the god himself. The same holds for the linguistic work. In the tragedy nothing is staged or displayed theatrically, but the battle of the new gods against the old is being fought. The linguistic work, originating in the speech of the people, does not refer to this battle; it transforms the people's saying so that now every living word fights the battle and puts up for decision what is holy and what unholy, what great and what small, what brave and what cowardly, what lofty and what flighty, what master and what slave (p. 43).

1. Martin Heidegger, *Poetry, Language, Thought*, trans. Albert Hofstadter (New York: Harper & Row, 1975), pp. 46–47.

On first glance we seem to be bordering here on the old familiar idea, deriving from Schiller, of the naiveté of the ancients: that is, the marvelous ability of ancient man to enter directly *into* nature—having never been separated from it—and to see his gods in his images, and his purposes in his gods. But if Heidegger's idea were based on something so nostalgic it would not help us with the problem of the motive behind impersonation. If we take this romantic interpretation of the passage, obvious problems arise: Did this capacity to "let the god himself be present" cease when the gods disappeared from the text and the subject of the tragedy became the fighting of earthly battles? Was the hero who came after the god "present" in the same way, and after the hero, the merchant and the courtesan and the braggart soldier? Or does this capacity imply a special and solemn belief, as in the Christian's belief that he is consuming the body of Christ in the holy sacrament? Does it diminish—this presence—as the pleasure principle displaces the spiritual principle in drama?

What Heidegger means here is not a literal presence of the god, but a presence that makes it unnecessary to refer elsewhere *for* the god. It is the *truth* of the god that arrives on the stage and not the stage that refers to a *real* god beyond it, existing in some unavailable form.[2] But we must not take this word *truth* in a vacant and abstract sense. In fact, the point Heidegger is making has

2. Hegel's explanation of this phenomenon: " [The gods] are made, invented, but are not fictitious. They certainly come forth out of the human imagination in contrast to what actually exists, but they do this as *essential* forms, and this product of the mind is at the same time recognized as being what is essential" (*Hegel on Tragedy,* eds. Anne and Henry Paolucci [New York: Harper & Row, 1975], p. 312).

nothing to do with gods at all. The same principle of presence applies to Van Gogh's painting of the peasant shoes. We know these are not real peasant shoes, and they are not painted substitutes for peasant shoes elsewhere. But that is an irrelevant factor, for it is not a matter of our vision shuttling back and forth between memory and pigment. It is obvious that we recognize these forms as shoes, but that does not mean that we consciously refer to a shoe-concept somewhere else, or earlier, or to something packed up in the mind's closet of known things. Everything about the painting forestalls such a movement of mind and draws us, as Heidegger says, into its "riff." "In the vicinity of the work we are suddenly somewhere else than we usually tend to be" (p. 35). This "somewhere else" is not a spatial elsewhere in the sense that the mind thinks of being elsewhere (*with* the real god, or *in* the room with the real shoes in the painting, or *on* this landscape Constable has "copied" in his painting), but in the sense that what is before us, the painting itself, offers a different kind of *here* than we "usually tend to be" in. The painting is a place of disclosure, not a place of reference. What is disclosed cannot be found elsewhere because it does not exist outside the painting. Hints of the painting exist in nature perhaps. When we next look at a pair of worn shoes we will see the "equipmental" qualities Van Gogh painted, but how is it that we did not see them before? The painting—shades of Oscar Wilde!— has perhaps altered our perception of reality. It does not make sense to say that all of the qualities of the shoes in Van Gogh's painting are in the real peasant shoes. Shoes are constantly being repainted by painters as possessing different qualities from those Van Gogh saw. Do these real shoes I am wearing, for example, possess qualities to be found in other shoe paintings I have never seen? If all of these qualities are in the shoes now, some of them dormantly waiting to be uncovered by future shoe painters, then we live in a very odd universe. Plainly there is something deficient about the referential principle as a basis of art.

It would be as absurd to argue that there is no referential, or mimetic, relation between art and reality as it is to argue that art is an imitation of reality. My purpose in presenting Heidegger's view here is not to restrict the nature of art's truth (or truths), or to endorse this particular view above others, but, as Heidegger would say, to open a clearing within the topic of art itself where we can be free of certain biases of the mimetic theory. The longstanding problem of mimetic theory is that it is obliged to define art in terms of what it is not, to seek *a source* of artistic representation in the subject matter of art, and to point to a place where it can be found, if only in a set of abstract ideas or truths, or in some field of essences or archetypes. The most important sentence ever written about drama, Aristotle's definition of tragedy as the imitation of an action, contains the whole range of mimetic theory's frustrations and ambiguity. These two virtually co-reflexive terms, *imitation* and *action,* come at us, in John Webster's figure, like two chained bullets. In one sense the term *imitation of* implies that the action is outside the drama, "a form," as John Jones says, "which the tragedian contemplates, and it stands logically and chronologically before the business of composition."[3] But in another sense, the term *action* seems to want to refer to some-

3. John Jones, *On Aristotle and Greek Tragedy* (New York: Oxford University Press, 1968), p. 24.

thing inside the play, an "indwelling form," a "soul," an "order of events," etc., and so the term *imitation* takes on a second character as the medium in which the work presents its representation. Could we have it both ways, prior to and concurrent with, inside and outside? I do not see why not. It seems unreasonable to try to repeal a history as interesting as that of our revisions of this endlessly fascinating sentence. What does seem important is that when we read the sentence one way or another we do not fall under the illusion that we are scientists reaching the correct solution to the problem. And so it is with phenomenological description: it is only a means of going all the way to the end of one of art's self-contradicting paths.

If my book has an even distantly polemical cast it is to be found in its neighborly reaction to semiotics, which is mimetic theory's most thriving relative. This may seem an odd gathering of clan but in the present context we might define semiotics as the scientific analysis of the means, or apparatus, of the mimetic process. In other words, what mimetic theory and semiotics, and the criticisms respectively derived from them, have in common is that they see theater as a process of mediation between artist and culture, speaker and listener; theater becomes a passageway for a cargo of meanings being carried back to society (after artistic refinement) via the language of signs. I do not see this as a deficiency of the semiotic enterprise; it is simply its particular project. One could no more expect semiotics to talk about anything else than one could have expected New Criticism, in its day, to talk about the neurosis of the play's hero or the author's autobiographical presence in his work. The fact is, any critical perspective is doomed to be narrow. It must be itself with a vengeance if it is to realize its potential for illumination. What is disturbing, if anything, about semiotics is not its narrowness but its almost imperialistic confidence in its product: that is, its implicit belief that you have exhausted a thing's interest when you have explained how it works as a sign.

The problem with semiotics is that in addressing theater as a system of codes it necessarily dissects the perceptual impression theater makes on the spectator. And, as Merleau-Ponty has said, "It is impossible . . . to decompose a perception, to make it into a collection of sensations, because in it the whole is prior to the parts."[4] Moreover, the more one treats theater as a language the more like *all* languages it becomes. Thus the danger of a linguistic approach to theater is that one is apt to look past the site of our sensory engagement with its empirical objects. This site is the point at which art is no longer *only* language. When the critic posits a division in the art image, he may be saying something about language, but he is no longer talking about art, or at least about the affective power of art.

This seems to me the primary limitation of a strictly semiotic perspective as we find it being applied to the study of theater. It is perhaps best expressed by Sigurd Burckhardt's idea that "the nature and primary function of the most important poetic devices"—among which we could include the devices of the theater—"is to release words in some measure from their bondage

4. Maurice Merleau-Ponty, *The Primacy of Perception and Other Essays on Phenomenological Psychology, the Philosophy of Art, History and Politics,* ed. James M. Edie (Evanston, Ill.: Northwestern University Press, 1964), p. 15.

to meaning, their purely referential role, and to give or restore to them the corporeality which a true medium needs."[5] In other words, what speech would be *saying,* in Burckhardt's sense, is that it isn't so much a carrier of a content (a story, a signified) as a medium that can only be animated by a content.

Even so, it seems to me that semiotics is a useful, if incomplete, discipline. It has become evident to me, in arriving at my own form of narrowness, that semiotics and phenomenology are best seen as complementary perspectives on the world and on art. I would like to pursue this notion further because there are times when I can be caught, so to speak, borrowing my neighbor's tools to build my own structures. If we think of semiotics and phenomenology as modes of seeing, we might say that they constitute a kind of binocular vision: one eye enables us to see the world phenomenally; the other eye enables us to see it significatively. These are the abnormal extremes of our normal vision. Lose the sight of your phenomenal eye and you become a Don Quixote (everything is something else); lose the sight of your significative eye and you become Sartre's Roquentin (everything is nothing but itself). Certainly the significative is the stronger—or at least the steadier—eye, which is to say that we tend to see the world as something we *get through.* But now and then the world detains us. For example: I am walking to the bus terminal to get my ride home. Suddenly, as I approach, the bus parked in the lot strikes me as being outrageously large and rectangular. It is heavy with material and texture; it is not a

5. Sigurd Burckhardt, *Shakespearean Meanings* (Princeton, N.J.: Princeton University Press, 1968), p. 24.

bus, it is a queer, unforeseen shape. This may be the result of the sun coming off it in a certain way, it may be my mood; but I find myself arrested by this *thing*. I see it almost as an artist might: as a study in form. But I must get on the bus if I am to make it home. So I climb aboard, with the help of my significative eye, and I project myself home—is there any mail? Did the plumber come today? What's for dinner? All of these anticipations are softened, however, because on the bus I read a news-paper, which is another way of not being where I am.

This is perhaps too personal an analogy, but by it I wish to express only the everyday nature of perceptual extremes: the thing, one might say, when it loses its lostness and appears before me, stripped of its func-tions; and the thing in its transportational value—its utility, what it means, what this strange/familiar thing will do for me. In its special way art is made of a fusion of these extremes. Actually, this a very old idea, for we are simply using modern terms and modern instances to restate a proposition of Horace: Poetry blends in one the delightful and the useful. Horace's meaning of the word "useful" *(utile)* is probably not in need of modern redefinition, but we must update the word "delightful" *(dulce)* if we are to make the point clear. Delight, it seems to me, could be translated as *wrappedness* in the image—not, as Dr. Johnson would say, for its "just gesture and elegant modulation,"[6] or for its successful

6. Samuel Johnson, *The Works of Samuel Johnson* (Oxford: W. Pickering, 1825), 5:121. The context of the quotation is: "The truth is, that the spectators are always in their senses, and know, from the first act to the last, that the stage is only a stage, and that the players are only players. They came to hear a certain number of lines re-cited with just gesture and elegant modulation."

execution of conventional usage, but for its autono-
mous life, or *liveliness* (to use a word particularly perti-
nent to theater). Thus there is a playful tug-of-war in
the image between the useful and the delightful. Usefulness implies the image's transitivity, its sign-ness, or
convertability into social, moral, or educational energy; delight implies its "corporeality" and the immediate absorption of the image by the senses. So the
sign/image is a Janus-faced thing: it wants to say something about something, to be a sign, and it wants to be
something, a thing in itself, a site of beauty. Blissfully
ignorant of the problems of deep structure, Horace
simply called this a blend of functions, no more sepa-
rable than body and soul, no more explainable by a
science of language than architecture is explainable
by the sciences of physics and engineering.

Perhaps two modern variations of this tension, concerned with very different projects, will illustrate its
persistence as a way of organizing our perspectives on
the image. I am immediately reminded of Baudelaire's
opposition of the significative (or ordinary) comic and
the absolute (or grotesque) comic: the ordinary comic is
always useful, "its element being visibly *double*—art and
the moral idea"; the absolute comic "comes much closer
to nature" and "emerges as a *unity* which calls for the
intuition to grasp it."[7] Baudelaire is concerned strictly
with "the essence" of laughter, but surely it would not be
stretching his polarity too far to see a generic connection
between laughter and delight; and one of the forms of

7. Charles Baudelaire, "On the Essence of Laughter," trans.
Jonathan Mayne, in *Comedy: Meaning and Form,* ed. Robert Corrigan (San Francisco: Chandler, 1965), p. 458.

laughter is the delight we take in the image. It need not even be a laughing image. To move to my second instance: one of Roland Barthes's tasks was to dismantle the accretion of signs that forms the received world of our modern mythologies—that is, the shared and therefore invisible world—and to reconstruct it, as it were, from the inside out by arresting its signs in their purest imagistic state. Only such an imagination could have approached the photograph (in *Camera Lucida*) as an interplay of the *studium* and the *punctum*. The *studium* is what one perceives in a photograph as the result of one's cultural preparation, or "a certain training,"[8] whereby we become the makers and consumers of photographs carrying what one might call our pictorial mythologies—beautiful sunsets, polluted sunsets, the many moods of the city, children being themselves, animals being "almost human," the Smiths posing happily at the Grand Canyon. The *studium* is "always coded" (p. 51) and "always refers to a classical body of information" (pp. 25–26); it is, in short, what we know without knowing it, what we see without seeing it. The *punctum* is a much rarer element (all photos do not have a *punctum*) and, unless I am mistaken, the *punctum* constitutes, for Barthes, the personal value of the photograph and perhaps its value as a work of art. The *punctum* is what elevates the picture above its *studium,* above being simply what we expect. It is "the wound" made by a "detail" which "paradoxically, while remaining a 'detail,' . . . fills the whole picture"; it is, finally, a seeming "accident" or "cast of the dice" in which the photo seems "to annihi-

8. Roland Barthes, *Camera Lucida: Reflections on Photography,* trans. Richard Howard (New York: Hill and Wang, 1982), p. 26.

late itself as a medium, to be no longer a sign but the thing itself" (p. 45).

These terms were designed strictly for the analysis of the photograph; but in essence they descend from the same vision I have been describing here. One of the things I deal with in this book (and a whole book could be written on the subject) is the passage of the stage image into conventionality, or sign-hood. I suggest that conventions occur first as anticonventions, or anti-signs (anti*studia* would do just as well): that is, to the extent that something is a convention, it is also a sign, meaning that it has taken its place as one of the efficient and invisible chips in the informational circuitry. But how did it get there in the first place if not as an attempt to *break into* the circuit, to pester the circuit with nuance, to *wound* it with the resistance of its presence? In other words, it began as an image in which the known world was, in some sense, being recreated or revised out of its primal linguistic matter.[9] In some such way all images, to one degree or another, erupt delightfully and claim their presence as a site of disclosure, putting us "somewhere else than we usually tend to be." Without this character as site, there *is* no delight, only the passage of information.

---

9. As another instance of this same passage, here is James L. Calderwood on the life cycle of the metaphor: "Each successful new metaphor is a creative insight and for a time gives off a spark of aesthetic pleasure. So long as tension exists between tenor and vehicle—so long as there is an element of the negative in our awareness that is not what it literally claims to be—the metaphor remains metaphoric. With wear, however, this tension slackens, and the metaphor collapses into an inert name—or more familiarly 'dies'" (*Metadrama in Shakespeare's Henriad: Richard II to Henry V* [Berkeley and Los Angeles: University of California Press, 1979], p. 14).

This phenomenal renewal is what, in my view, keeps the life in theater. In this pursuit, no doubt, theater belongs with all art, but its peculiar way of belonging is what I have tried to examine in these essays. In point of its organization, the book is divided into two parts titled (with a nod to Kenneth Burke's famous "ratios") *The Scene* and *The Actor.* These are really two perspectives from which theater can be viewed rather than two separate subjects. I take it that we can consider them as fundamental perspectives in the sense that Molière spoke of the theater as consisting of a platform (a scene) and a couple of passions (actors). Looking at theater as *scene* I am interested primarily in its way of using the tools of speech and carpentry to create a world. Obviously, the tool of speech puts us immediately on the ground of Part 2 (*The Actor*), but here I am considering the actor strictly as scene maker and not as performer. In the first chapter ("The World on Stage") I develop the idea that theater is a rather predatory institution that not only holds a mirror up to nature but consumes nature as well. It may be an unflattering figure, but the more I have thought about theater the more I see it as having the characteristics of an organism: it feeds on the world as its nourishment, it adapts to cultural climate and conditions that necessitate periodic shifts in direction and speed, and finally it exhausts itself and dies—one of its traditions, like generations, replacing another. Chapter 1 is an overview dealing mainly, one might say, with food gathering; chapters 2 and 3 present a more or less anatomical view of three major species of theater: the poetic stage of Shakespeare and the practical stage of naturalism (chapter 2), and the experimental theater that has dominated this century since the advent of expressionism (chapter 3).

Viewing theater from the standpoint of *the actor,* we encounter a very different set of phenomenological problems. We are not in the least interested in the psychology of the actor (how he prepares, what he thinks and feels while acting, and so on) but in the psychology—if that is the best word—of the audience viewing the actor. We want to know what we see *in* and *through* the actor as the instrument on which the text of the play is performed. Chapter 1 ("Actor/Text") is concerned mainly with the presence of the actor on stage and the question of his essential influence on the dramatist (how, for example, does the fiction written for the actor differ from one written for a reader?). Chapter 2 ("Actor/Audience") treats acting as a form of speech addressed to an audience. That is, on the textual side the actor creates the conditions that define the limits of theater as an art form; on the audience side he makes theater occur. As speaker, the actor may be *listened to* in different ways; we may hear and see him in different keys of perception (what significance is there, for example, in the fact that the actor speaks to be overheard but speaks as if he *weren't* being overheard?). In any case, this final chapter, ending in a brief phenomenology of the curtain call, is less about the art of acting than about the complex act of seeing and hearing the actor as a kind of healthy schizophrenic who is living two lives at the same time.

It has occurred to me, in fact, that most of the book was written from a theater seat in my mind's eye. As a consequence, it is quite possible that an actor or a director reading it will find some of its assumptions naive in exactly the sense that poets frequently find readers' interpretations of their work wrong or "not at all what was intended"—or, "not at all what we *do* in the theater or *how* we do what we do." An Actor—I keep hearing a mythical actor say—would *not* think of Lear's "Blow winds" as a dangerous speech (one of my claims). "He would simply do it, and that's that!" I certainly hope so. But in my theater seat I am waiting for this speech because it is a big one and I want the actor to be up to it. He is in danger here of failing to be Lear, and I would assume that if he *thinks* about this while doing the speech, he is probably already deeply in the remote danger I see as being both the risk and the perceptual thrill of his art.

Finally, I must warn the reader that Prince Hamlet seems to lurk around every corner in this latter half of the book. At one point I thought of following the example of Kierkegaard in *The Concept of Irony, with Constant Reference to Socrates* and somehow sneaking Hamlet into my title, as if he had been part of my plan all along. Since this proved awkward and entirely transparent, I will only offer a brief plea for my reader's patience with the terrible truth: my addiction to the play. I have never been able to resist poking about in *Hamlet* for the secrets of Shakespeare's art. For me, it is the greatest playwright's greatest play, and though I don't necessarily expect the reader to share that view, I trust that what I say about it can be generously applied, where appropriate, to all the other plays I might have used to illustrate my ideas.

Part One

The Scene

1

The World on Stage

If we approach theater semiotically we must surely agree with the Prague linguists that "all that is on the stage is a sign,"[1] and that anything deliberately put there for artistic purposes becomes a sign when it enters illusionary space and time. That is, it becomes an event in a self-contained illusion outside the world of social praxis but conceptually referring to that world in some way, if only in the fact that the illusion is *about* hypothetical human beings. As long as there is pretense, or playing, there is pretense *of* something, and this *of* constitutes a bridge between the stage and its fictional analogue of the world, or, if you wish, between the sign and its various significations.[2]

However, if we approach theater phenomenologically there is more to be said. For, among other consider-

1. Jiri Veltrusky, "Man and Object in the Theater," in *A Prague School Reader on Esthetics, Literary Structure, and Style,* ed. Paul L. Garvin (Washington: Georgetown University Press, 1964), p. 84.

2. In strictly Saussurian terms, the signifier and the signified are indivisible aspects of the sign. Yet some protostructuralists of Prague were more interested in the referential connection between language and the world than is generally supposed, and their work was, to some extent, phenomenologically inspired. (See, for example, Veltrusky's prefatory remarks to *Drama as Literature* [Lisse: The Peter de Ridder Press, 1977], where he explains that studies pub-

ations, there is a sense in which signs, or certain kinds of signs, or signs in a certain stage of their life cycle, achieve their vitality—and in turn the vitality of theater—not simply by signifying the world but by being *of* it. In other words, the power of the sign—or, as I will refer to it here, the image—is not necessarily exhausted either by its illusionary or its referential character. This may be obvious enough in itself, but some implications of the idea seem important enough to develop beyond the semiotic notion that such images are simply signs with a high degree of "iconic identity."[3] But putting semiotics aside, we tend generally to undervalue the elementary fact that theater—unlike fiction, painting, sculpture, and film—is really a language whose words consist to an unusual degree of things that *are* what they seem to be. In theater, image and object, pretense and pretender, sign-vehicle and content, draw unusually close. Or, as Peter Handke more interestingly puts it, in the theater light is brightness pretending to be other brightness, a chair is a chair pretending to be another chair, and so on.[4] Put bluntly, in theater there is always a possibility that an act of sexual congress between two so-called signs will produce a real pregnancy.

lished under Nazi occupation could not acknowledge indebtedness to Husserl and Ingarden, among others.) This is also the case, as the reader will see, with a supposedly Saussurian semiologist like Roland Barthes. In this study I am less interested in the linguistic constitution of the sign than I am in the relationship of the sign (or image) and what Peirce terms the *referent,* or the reality denoted by the sign.

3. Keir Elam, *The Semiotics of Theatre and Drama* (London: (Methuen & Co., 1980), p. 22.

4. Peter Handke, *Kaspar and Other Plays,* trans. Michael Roloff (New York: Farrar, Straus and Giroux, 1969), p. 10.

It comes down, of course, to a matter of perspective. Quite legitimately, to the extent that something is *not* a sign the semiotician would lose interest in it, since he is concerned only with the sign-ness of things, and what they do in their spare time is their own (or someone else's) business. And quite legitimately, the phenomenologist, in pursuit of "the essence" of things, will subsume their sign function—along with all other possible functions—under their phenomenal character as objects in the real world.[5] Of course, the literary critic may complacently ignore both of these concerns in his quest of the theme or the style or the historical import of any set of art images. All are, as it were, workers in the same field harvesting different kinds of crops.

By way of establishing my own perspective, it will be useful to begin with a well-known definition of art by Victor Shklovsky that will serve as a departing point for much of what I have to say in this chapter:

Art exists that one may recover the sensation of life; it exists to make one feel things, to make the stone *stony.* The purpose of art is to impart the sensation of things as they are perceived and not as they are known. The technique of art is to make objects "unfamiliar," to make forms difficult, to increase the difficulty and length of perception because the process of perception is an aesthetic end in itself and must be prolonged. *Art is a way of experiencing the artfulness of an object; the object is not important.*[6]

5. Throughout, I use the adjective *phenomenal* in the sense of pertaining to phenomena or to our sensory experience with empirical objects. The adjective *phenomenological,* of course, refers to the analytical or descriptive problem of dealing with such phenomena.

6. Victor Shklovsky, "Art as Technique," in *Russian Formalist Criticism: Four Essays,* trans. Lee T. Lemon and Marion J. Reis (Lincoln: University of Nebraska Press, 1965), p. 12. Italics Shklovsky's.

Such a concept of art arises from, or at least leans into, the phenomenological attitude. Here art is perceived as an act of removing things from a world in which they have become inconspicuous and seeing them anew. Perhaps it would be better to say "seeing them as of old," for the presumption behind Shklovsky's theory is that we grow away, perceptually, from the contents of reality (habit being a great deadener) and that art is a way of bringing us home via an "unfamiliar" route. This much, at least, art has in common with phenomenological reduction: if art is a way of endowing the world with meaning it is also a way of allowing the world to express itself. If the objects of reality depicted in art carry some of their worldly meanings with them—and no one would deny that they do—they are now seen, by a trick of perspective, to have been partially concealed all along *by* the meanings. The meanings, instead of preceding the objects (as eye glasses

---

It should be said that Shklovsky (as the last sentence in the quotation might suggest) does not see artfulness as an end in itself but as a means of rediscovering the object in its uniqueness. The thrust of his idea is almost interchangeable with Heidegger's concept (developed after Shklovsky's) of the "founding of truth" in the art work. For example: "The setting-into-work of truth thrusts up the unfamiliar and extraordinary and at the same time thrusts down the ordinary and what we believe to be such. The truth that discloses itself in the work can never be proved or derived from what went before. What went before is refuted in its exclusive reality by the work. What art founds can therefore never be compensated and made up for by what is already present and available. Founding is an overflow, an endowing, a bestowal" ("The Origin of the Work of Art," in *Poetry, Language, and Truth,* trans. Albert Hofstadter [New York: Harper & Row, 1975], p. 75).

precede vision), now trail them, like the tails of comets. The object comes forth, as in the trunks and limbs of Van Gogh's olive trees, and we experience "the unmotivated upsurge of the world."[7] As the phenomenologist would say, the object becomes "self-given," and "something can be *self-given* only if it is no longer given merely through any sort of symbol; in other words, only if it is not 'meant' as the mere 'fulfillment' of a sign which is previously defined in some way or other. In this sense, *phenomenological* philosophy is a continual *desymbolization of the world.*"[8]

If we now come back to Shklovsky's idea that art imparts "the sensation of things as they are perceived and not as they are known," we see how the phenomenological attitude differs from the semiotic in its descriptive yield. Here is a possible basis for a distinction between *image* and *sign*. Let us agree that either term can be said to contain the other and that either can be defined in many ways, as we see in moving from relatively simple theories of the sign (Sartre, Rudolf Arnheim, the dictionary) to highly complex ones (Peirce, Husserl, Derrida). In any case, the term *sign* is, in itself, a sign of the semiotic attitude, which is heavily dialectical (or, in Peirce's case, triadic): the referential urgency of the word *sign* is reproduced in its sub-, or correlative terms—signifier and signified—one of which always forms the background of intelligibility of the other. To speak of the signifier is already to begin gossiping

7. Maurice Merleau-Ponty, *Phenomenology of Perception,* trans. Colin Smith (New York: Humanities Press, 1970), p. xiv.

8. Max Scheler, *Selected Philosophical Essays,* trans. David R. Lachterman (Evanston, Ill.: Northwestern University Press, 1973), p. 143.

about a signified, to be thrown back into an elsewhere of assignable meaning. In adopting the more aesthetic term *image*—as any likeness, or representation, made out of the materials of the medium (gesture, language, decor, sound, light[9])—I am under no illusion that I am freeing myself of the dialectical problem, nor am I denying that an image signifies (is an image of something) or hauls behind it, in Peirce's term, an "infinite semiosis"; I am merely trying to abridge the process of signification and throw the emphasis onto the empathic response. In the image, one might say, we swallow the semiotic process whole and imagination catches its disease. It is the disease that interests the phenomenologist, not the germ that causes it or the stages of its progress.[10]

Or let us take Shklovsky's idea that art makes objects "unfamiliar" (a statement, incidentally, that allows us to ground revolutions like Brecht's in an aesthetic orthodoxy[11]). Art increases difficulty and length of perception. By difficulty, of course, Shklovsky is not referring

9. For convenience, I am excluding here the equally valid meaning of image as the picture thrown on the retina by any object, in or out of art. In this sense, of course, the word *image* is universally applicable to anything one sees.

10. Paul Ricoeur: "One can present phenomenology as a generalized theory of language. Language ceases to be an activity, a function, an operation among others: it is identified with the entire signifying milieu, with the complex of signs thrown like a net over our field of perception, our action, our life" (*The Conflict of Interpretations,* ed. Don Ihde [Evanston, Ill.: Northwestern University Press, 1974], p. 247).

11. On this point, see Terence Hawkes, *Structuralism and Semiotics* (Berkeley and Los Angeles: University of California Press, 1977), pp. 62–63.

to stylistic obscurity but to expressive density. The image detains, arrests. It carries, in Gaston Bachelard's splendid word, its own *exaggeration,* which imagination "seizes" and carries, sensationally, to its "ultimate extreme."[12] Unlike the sign, the image is unique and unreproducible (except as facsimile); whereas the sign is of no value unless it repeats itself; in fact, as Derrida says, "a sign which does not repeat itself, which is not already divided by repetition in its 'first time', is not a sign."[13] In other words, the inclination of the sign is to become more efficient, to be read easily. In the strictly utilitarian sphere (which of course does not exhaust signification) the sign gets down to its referential business with as little flourish as possible: for example, the red STOP signal or the trousered silhouette on the men's room door (really an icon). But if this inclination applied as strictly to plays and their images, we could cut a great deal of the text of *Macbeth,* or even reduce it, allegorically, to the sign of a dagger with a diagonal red line across it. But Macbeth is extremely "difficult" or inefficient, taken as a sign. The proof of this is not in its significative subtlety but in the fact that the play does far more than is necessary in order to mean whatever it may mean (the history of a Scottish king, a study in crime and punishment). It is, in addition, a sensory experience that cannot be accounted for by semiotic systems (for instance, Peirce's threefold classification of predominantly iconic, indexical

12. Gaston Bachelard, *The Poetics of Space,* trans. Maria Jolas (Boston: Beacon Press, 1969), pp. 219–20.
13. Jacques Derrida, "The Theater of Cruelty and the Closure of Representation," in *Writing and Difference,* trans. Alan Bass (Chicago: University of Chicago Press, 1978), p. 246.

and symbolic signs, or Barthes's hermeneutic, semantic, proairetic, cultural, and symbolic codes). As a single illustration, take the opening lines of Macbeth's soliloquy:

> If it were done when 'tis done, then 'twere well
> It were done quickly.
>
> *(I, vii, 1–2)*

These words certainly express the collision of Macbeth's hesitation and momentum: behind the words stands the moral man in conflict with his own ambition. But this is not why an actor wants to "speak the speech" or why, hearing it, we are thrilled by it, or why it is one of the most fondled moments of the play. It is, phenomenally, a unique claim staked on speech by sound, as if the sound *done* possessed a powerful instinct of self-preservation. Here, in fact, repetition conjures the endlessness of sound's very utility (three usages constitute a pattern, and a pattern is a potential infinity). In short, sound is not consumed in its sense: sound simply gives in to language, as marble gives in to the chisel; it consents to be the ground of a possible expressiveness. Finally, no semantic explanation— such as that sense is passing through sound, or that sound and sense are inextricable—can exhaust the marvel of what is left under: the fact that the body, in possessing the sound, is "gripped" by its vibrations; we can say of *done* what Merleau-Ponty says of the German word *rot* (red): it "pushes its way through my body. I have the feeling, difficult to describe, of a kind of numbed fullness which invades my body, and which at the same time imparts to my mouth cavity a spherical shape."[14] And so with the entire play: from the stand-point of its musical code—or should we say visceral code?—it is a field of sound (just as, in the scenic connection, it is a field of space and shape) in which meanings parasitically swarm.

Granted, this is a deeply subjective reduction. More than anything else, I am trying to "exaggerate" the medium of theater, its affective corporeality as the carrier of meanings. Primarily, the line *means* something: it comes out of the mouth of a character in a play about murder and its consequences; Macbeth is the image of a hypothetical man. And here we uncover another root difference between sign and image, stated most simply by Sartre: "The material of the sign is totally indifferent to the object it signifies. . . . But the relationship between the material of the physical image and its object is altogether different; the two *resemble* each other."[15] And a further implication immediately relevant to theater: "In every image, even in the one which does not posit that its subject exists, there is a positional determination. In the sign, as such, this determination is lacking. . . . The sign . . . does not deliver its object" (pp. 29–30). Here we arrive at the source of the peculiar "difficulty" of stage images: the sense, for example, of Macbeth being *here* before us yet absent, of his story being unreal but imprisoned "positionally" in real time and space. Moreover, the particular density of the theater image rests in the fact that the whole perceptual ensemble of theater introduces a resistance to the gath-

14. Merleau-Ponty, *Phenomenology of Perception,* p. 236.
15. Jean-Paul Sartre, *The Psychology of Imagination,* trans. Bernard Frechtman (New York: Washington Square Press, 1968), p. 27.

ering of certain levels of meaning. If you were interested in *Macbeth* for the density of its significations, it
would be better to stay home and read the text—not, as
it is often said, because reading affords the leisure to go
back and ponder (though this is obviously a factor), but
because reading presents almost no phenomenal distraction. In one respect, a play read and enacted in the
mind's eye is more "real" than one seen on stage. By
"real" I mean nothing palpable or objectively real, obviously, but only that our mental enactment of *Macbeth*,
however vague or fleeting, has something of the realism of a succession of dream images; it is an imagined
actual experience that floats wherever the text leads. In
a reading, everything is susceptible to envisionment;
the mind may suddenly lose its image of Macbeth
speaking and see only his "multitudinous seas incarna-
dine" or the "naked new born babe" striding the blast
of his imagination. But however fantastic or surreal the
image, it is all real in the sense of its springing to an
imagined actuality. Whereas a theatrical presentation
of the text is precisely marked by the limits of artifice:
the frontal rigidity of our view, the positional determination of everything on stage, the condensation of
Macbeth into a real form, the fact that the play has already passed through the screen of an interpretation by
director and actors.

Naturally what literary critics study so assiduously is
their own dreamed text of the play, and for this reason
their interpretations have a way of treating Macbeth as a
once (and still) real man whose life, thanks to Shakespeare, is an open book. It is because words on the page
have no resemblance to the things they conjure that

reading is such a transparent process. In reading, the eye is an anesthetized organ, little more than a window to the waiting consciousness on which a world of signification imprints itself with only the barest trace of the signifiers that carry it. In the theater, however, the eye awakens and confiscates the image. What the text loses in significative power in the theater it gains in corporeal presence, in which there is extraordinary perceptual satisfaction. Hence the need for rounding out a semiotics of the theater with a phenomenology of its imagery—or, if you will, a phenomenology of its semiology.

Let us begin at rock bottom with some instances of things that resist being either signs or images, at least in the sense that we have discussed them to this point. This may be difficult to document convincingly because we all have different capacities for settling into the theater illusion. Moreover, it is a simple fact that almost anything, under the right sociological conditions, can be "seen through" and pass into convention, the most outrageous being the convention of real blood in the Roman gladiatorial games. What we are trying to catch here, in Bachelard's words, is "the original amazement of a naive observer." And, as he adds immediately, "Amazement of this kind is rarely felt twice. Life quickly wears it down."[16] To this end, I have chosen a few things that have abnormal durability and might illustrate the idea that stage images (including actors) do not always or entirely surrender their objective nature to the sign/image function. They retain, in other words, a high degree of *en soi.*

16. Bachelard, *The Poetics of Space,* p. 107.

I take the first from Walter Benjamin's essay, "The Work of Art in the Age of Mechanical Reproduction." "A clock that is working," Benjamin says, "will always be a disturbance on the stage. . . .Even in a naturalistic play, astronomical time would clash with theatrical time."[17] I doubt that such a clash would really occur in a naturalistic play in which theatrical time and real time were roughly identical. Why, then, do stage designers usually take the precaution of removing the minute hand or masking the clock face? Clearly, there is something about a working clock on stage that is minimally disturbing to an audience. But it has less to do with time per se than with our awareness that theatrical time is being measured by a real clock—an instrument that is visibly obeying its own laws of behavior. I doubt that this would be a very serious distraction, or would remain one for very long, or that a certain kind of theater project couldn't take advantage of a working clock heeding its own rhythms. I am simply saying that some things, by virtue of their nature, retain an exceptional degree of self-givenness on a stage. A better case might be made for fire or running water. A working fountain, for example, is mildly distracting, in the sense of being "interesting." It is not that circulating water (like fire) is a threat to the illusion, as would a glass of water accidentally spilled by an actor; in fact, it has been a standard enhancement of theatrical spectacle for a long time. But it is the sort of detail one would remember in describing the setting to others because real water—unlike real chairs, clothing, flower vases, or the painted

17. Walter Benjamin, *Illuminations,* ed. Hannah Arendt (New York: Schocken Books, 1977), p. 247.

façades of a village square—retains a certain primal strangeness: its aesthetic function does not exhaust its interest. It is a happening taking place within the aesthetic world: with running water something indisputably real leaks out of the illusion.

An even better example is the child actor. Who has ever seen a child on stage without thinking, "How well he acts, for a child!" or, of the doomed children in *Medea,* "Do they *understand* the play?" No doubt Elizabethan audiences at Paul's and Blackfriars got used to seeing children in adult roles and, to some extent, saw them only conventionally, as they saw male actors (often boys) playing female roles. But the children's troupes did not carry away "Hercules and his load" because they were magnificent actors. Their success— their *raison d'être*—depended heavily on the audience's "double vision," even to the point that the companies specialized in comedy and satire, the genres most closely linked to any audience's immediate world. Moreover, unlike the adult companies, they were permitted exceptional license in abusing the audience, including royalty in it. Various explanations have been offered for this privileged status, among them the "inherent innocence" of children, but Michael Shapiro is surely right in saying, in his book on the boy companies, that it comes down to "the disparity between the actors and their roles."[18] We can expand this idea, phenomenologically, by adding that it would have been a waste of a good thing to confine children to the acting

18. Michael Shapiro, *Children of the Revels: The Boy Companies of Shakespeare's Time and Their Plays* (New York: Columbia University Press, 1977), p. 107.

of tragedies and serious plays that depended on a suspension of disbelief—something adult companies could have satisfied much more easily. But in comedy and satire, where actors spend a good deal of time flirting with the audience, children would be in their element. The point is not so much that they are children but that they are conspicuously *not* identical with their characters. As a consequence, the medium becomes the message: the form winks at the content. So one might say that the purpose of the abuse was not to be abusive at the audience's expense, but to carry to perfection the titillating potential of a medium that by its very nature innoculates the audience *against* belief; paradoxically, the abuse is distanced (made genial) by the fact that it is openly indulged by "actors" flaunting their "insincerity"—all of which reminds us that satire is probably most vicious when it is tucked surreptitiously into the illusion (e.g., the "Politic Would-Be" plot of *Volpone*), where its sincerity can become deafening.

Finally, we come down to the stage animal. An animal can be trained or tranquilized, but it cannot categorically be depended upon. There is always the fact that it doesn't know it is in a play; consequently, we don't get good behavior, only behavior. Here we have a case in which strangeness, for both actor and audience, can be the occasion of either nervousness or delight. In a sense, the cat in Pinter's *The Collection* poses a bigger threat to the actress who is required to hold it through much of the play than a Bengal tiger poses for the lion tamer whose act depends on the gamble that the animal may go wild. Nonetheless, an animal following its own inclinations can be used to great effect on the stage. In productions of *Two Gentlemen of Verona* Launce's dog Crab usually steals the show by simply being itself. Anything the dog does—ignoring Launce, yawning, wagging its tail, forgetting its "lines"—becomes hilarious or cute because it is doglike. The effect here is comic because it is based on a *bisociation,* in Arthur Koestler's term.[19] We have an intersection of two independent and self-contained phenomenal chains—natural animal behavior and culturally programmed human behavior. The "flash" at the intersection, equivalent to the punch line of a joke, comes in our attributing human qualities to the dog (a wagging tail is a signal that the dog has understood; a yawn is a signal that it is bored); but beneath this is our conscious awareness that the dog is a real dog reacting to what, for it, is simply another event in its dog's life. So we have an instance of Bergson's comic formula in reverse: the living encrusts itself on the mechanical—mechanical here meaning the prefabricated world of the play. In short, we have a real dog on an artificial street.[20]

What surprises us, of course, is that the dog *can* be used in the play, that it unknowingly cooperates in creating the illusion. And this surprise arises from our observation of the dog as a dog-in-itself. Questions like this might occur: Isn't it interesting that the dog will submit to being on stage? Then, of course, the answer:

19. Arthur Koestler, *The Act of Creation* (New York: MacMillan, 1969), p. 45.
20. There is no evidence that a dog actually appeared in the role of Crab in the early history of *Two Gentlemen.* My argument here does not preclude the possibility that it might be equally funny to allow the actor to create an imaginary dog in the scene.

It *isn't* submitting, it is simply being itself. What if it barks? Urinates? Obviously, even these natural acts, like the abuse of the boy actors, would contribute to further comedy. So the illusion has suddenly become a field of play, of "what if?" The illusion has introduced something into itself to demonstrate its tolerance of *things*. It is not the world that has invaded the illusion; the illusion has stolen something from the world in order to display its own power. Finally, one also suspects that an element of self-parody enters the play with the dog. The whole enterprise of theatrical illusionism gets gently debunked, a freedom Shakespeare was fond of indulging (self-parody being one of the best proofs of humility). The theater has, so to speak, met its match: the dog is blissfully above, or beneath, the business of playing, and we find ourselves cheering its performance precisely because it isn't one.

Below these examples, of course, is the whole phenomenal floor of the theater illusion—the physical actuality of actor and stage—which, for the most part, we accept as perceptually given. My purpose has been to suggest points at which the floor cracks open and we are startled, however pleasantly, by the upsurge of the real into the magic circle where the conventions of theatricality have assured us that the real has been subdued and transcended. We suddenly see the familiar in the defamiliarization. The question now is: To what extent can these nodes of reality extruding from the illusion any longer be called images or signs? If an image, by definition, is a likeness or a representation of something, how can it be the thing itself? Again, our approach lies in the theater's special openness to the world of objects. A dog on stage is certainly an object (like the furniture that theater companies borrow from businessmen); but the act of theatricalizing it—putting it into an intentional space—neutralizes its objectivity and claims it as a *likeness* of a dog. Essentially it is the same process that occurs when a painter portrays an image of his dog on canvas, except that in the theater there is no ontological difference between the image and the object. Consider, as another example, Molière playing Molière in *The Impromptu of Versailles.* What fascinates us here is the Escheresque idea of the reverse *trompe-l'oeil:* the illusion spawning its own creator, thus positing an exception to the aesthetic rule that the image is not the thing. Of course, at bottom it is a false exception because Molière is *still* not Molière; or rather, he is Molière *plus* a Molière text, or Molière *minus* the freedom to "be himself." The phenomenal interest lies in the distance between the two Molières and the going back and forth of the mind's eye from one to the other. Or, to leave this form of theater and move to another, do we not, in some such way, see animals in the intentional space of a zoo as vaguely oscillating between animals and images or signs of animals? Even the name placard on the cage—"*DINGO*: Wild Dog of Australia . . ."—implies that the animal has been snared in its empirical wilderness and brought to this pseudosurrounding to serve as an illustration of what the real animal is like. The pedagogy of zooviewing says to us: "This is the *kind* of dog you would see in Australia." It is not in the least a question of the animal losing its actuality, but only of what perceptual change something undergoes when, as Cleopatra puts it (fearing a similar fate in Rome), it is "uplifted to the view." In other words, an object becomes a signifying, exemplary image only in a consciousness. We perceive the dog on the stage imaginatively, as we perceive the dog in the zoo indicatively. Therefore, in those moments when we see only the real dog rather than Launce's dog, our consciousness has simply slipped into another gear. We may see the dog as dog or as image, or we may allow our mind to oscillate rapidly between the two kinds of perception, as with the duck/rabbit sketch of the gestalt psychologists.

We arrive, inevitably, at something like a law of complementarity: to the extent that something on stage arouses awareness of its external (or workaday) significations, its internal (or illusionary) signification is reduced. On first glance, this would seem to be a proposition worthy of the First Gravedigger in *Hamlet*. It becomes more interesting, however, when one thinks how much theater is intentionally devoted to confusing these two orders of signification, if not trying to subjugate one to the power of the other. Such intentions imply no violation of the principle of illusion, only an enlargement of our idea of what illusion is with respect to its basis in the empirical world. And my thesis here is that the dog on the stage is a nearly perfect symptom of the cutting edge of theater, the bite that it takes into actuality in order to sustain itself in the dynamic order of its own ever-dying signs and images. One could define the history of theater—especially where we find it overthrowing its own traditions—as a progressive colonization of the real world. If I may use Artaud's words in a connection that would have appalled him, theater is a "re-conquest of the signs of what exists."[21] By this I do

21. Antonin Artaud, *The Theater and Its Double,* trans. Mary Caroline Richards (New York: Grove Press, 1958), p. 63.

not mean what Artaud had in mind, a theater that "ensnares the organs" through "cruelty," but a theater that brings us into phenomenal contact with *what exists*, or with what it is possible *to do*, theatrically, with what exists. If this concerned only such stubbornly real things as dogs (and children) it would be a negligible point at best. But the dog is simply at the lowest echelon of living things that come on stage tethered to the real world. By "living" I refer to things that are alive in the sense of belonging to immediate existence, to the steady flux of signs, but not yet to the world of art. It is, finally, a matter of gestation: theater ingests the world of objects and signs only to bring images to life. In the image, a defamiliarized and desymbolized object is "uplifted to the view" where· we see it as being phenomenally heavy with itself. A transitional moment of shock signals the onset of the image: one feels the shudder of its refusal to settle into the illusion. One might say that the force of its significations, felt all at once, overloads the artistic circuit, as in the filaments of those early light bulbs that glowed intensely with the first surge of power; it is perceived not as a signifier but as a signified, though phenomenologically speaking these words now pertain to an alien vocabulary since it is exactly signification that has been ingested.

I can perhaps bring these last remarks down to earth by adapting an idea from Nelson Goodman. In *Ways of Worldmaking* Goodman suggests that something may be a work of art on one occasion and not a work of art on another. It is not a question, he says, of *what* is art but *when* is art. A stone may be a quite utilitarian object in one's driveway and a work of art in a museum where attention is called to its symbolic qualities (shape, color, texture).[22] It is, then, the trip to the museum, and not necessarily technique, that makes the stone stony (to come back to Shklovsky). Can we say so quickly, however, that "all that is in the museum is a work of art" and be done with classification? Let us take a more ambiguous example, though one by now so familiar to museumgoers that it may be difficult to recapture its transition from object to image. Let us say we encounter a pile of rubble on the museum floor. Whether this mess has been created by an artist or by a careless custodian we have no way of knowing, but it is plainly showing off. Isn't the rubble optically saying something like this?

I am a work of art even though I am not one. I have nothing to commend myself as art except the fact that I have been dumped *here,* where you have been taught to see things artfully: here you see rubble *rubbly.* Unlike the fire extinguisher on the wall above me, I am art only because I seem to be advertised as art (why else am I here?), while the fire extinguisher is advertised only as a requirement of the safety code (though *my* presence in its vicinity perhaps makes you think twice about that). What I am, in fact, is not important. What is important is that I come from outside art: I hover between actuality and possibility; I am an unforeseen exaggeration of the matter of art.

In short, art is a certain perspective on substance.

There are few such exaggerated exaggerations in the theater. But the drive of theater—or, to acknowledge

22. Nelson Goodman, *Ways of Worldmaking* (Indianapolis, Ind.: Hackett Publishing Company, 1978), p.67.

its multiplicity of functions, *one* of its drives—derives from the "rubble" principle. In the theater we are, technically, within the museum: all that is on stage is art; but what enters the theater originates, so to speak, in the driveway outside. That is, among the various appetites of theater we find the need for a certain roughage of hard-core reality that continuously nourishes the illusionary system. One might describe the theater as an infinitely tolerant institution that can incorporate almost anything into its diet. And it is probably less through anthropological findings than through nostalgic stirrings that we have always thought of the early stage as having begun on the circular threshing floor on which the community's food was winnowed from nature. It does not matter whether this was in fact the case, only that the image of the threshing floor substantiates our feeling that there is a connection between theater, as ritual, and the symbolism of food. Beyond this, the significance of the circle is that it is the essential shape of all concentration, not only in optics but in physical nature as well (the centrifugal and centripetal forces, nature as a wearing off of sharp edges). But the special significance of the circle metaphor is that theater is the one place where society collects in order to look in upon itself as a third-personal other. Beneath all of the possible explanations of theater's usefulness as an image of man, there is this basic consubstantiality of form between its subject and its process. Theater (*theatron,* derived from "to see") is a means of looking objectively at the subjective life of the race as something prepared for the community out of the substance of its own body. Thus theater has the lineaments of a secular sacrifice in the implicit meaning of Grotowski's statement that the actor is not there *for* us but *instead of* us. Theater is the medium, par excellence, that consumes the real in its realest forms: man, his language, his rooms and cities, his weapons and tools, his other arts, animals, fire, and water—even, finally, theater itself. Its permanent spectacle is the parade of objects and processes *in transit* from environment to imagery.

There is a wonderful parable by Kafka, brought to my attention some years ago by a Geoffrey Hartman essay, that expresses this idea somewhat less carnivorously. In addition, it is an excellent model of the metamorphosis of the new theater image into the conventional formula.

Leopards break into the temple and drink the sacrificial chalices dry; this occurs repeatedly, again and again: finally it can be reckoned on beforehand and becomes part of the ceremony.[23]

Of course the temple is the theater and the leopards the reality outside, or what of reality has not yet been articulated in theatrical imagery but is, so to speak, prowling around in search of a way in. As an illustration from which we might derive a standard pattern that occurs over and again, let us take a basic image with a rather dramatic onset—one, moreover, that is one of the key moments of a massive shift in the mimetic possibilities of the modern stage.

In the early nineteenth-century French theater, as elsewhere in Europe, it was not the custom to furnish the

23. Geoffrey Hartman, "Structuralism: The Anglo-American Adventure," *Yale French Studies* 36–37 (1966): 167.

settings of serious plays—comedy, again is a somewhat different matter—but to paint chairs and tables on the wings and drops. First, there was the problem of adequate lighting to illuminate the upstage area; but furniture was basically useless anyway, except for a few indispensable pieces, because the infamous "downstage line" of the neoclassic era had firmly pinned the actors to a semicircle around the prompt box. But realism was already (or once again) in the air, and directors like Baron Taylor and (later) Montigny began insisting that the stage more nearly resemble the world. Montigny, for example, revolutionized what we now call blocking (in the early 1850s) by putting a table and chairs directly upstage of the prompt box as a way of forcing the actors out of the semicircle into more lifelike positions.[24] From all reports, this created a temporary frenzy among the actors, since the art of acting—or grand acting, at least—had never required skill in moving around household obstacles. (Perhaps only an actor can appreciate the seriousness of this problem.) One can only imagine how the first audiences reacted to this innovation. But one can guess that so much furniture, intruding insolently on this sacred space reserved by long tradition for the great set speeches of the drama, would not have been received simply as images and signs of chairs and tables belonging to the fictional world of the play but as *things* imported from the realm of the real, as unforeseen on the stage as the nude in Manet's *Le Déjeuner sur l'Herbe*. It goes without saying that practical furniture soon (be-

---

24. Marvin Carlson, "French Stage Composition from Hugo to Zola," *Educational Theatre Journal* 23 (December 1971): 368. I am greatly indebted to Professor Carlson for his research and advice on this period.

tween 1850 and 1870) lost whatever shock value it may
have had (unlike Manet's nude!) and was incorporated
into the illusion because, like Kafka's leopards, it kept
coming back: playwrights and directors kept producing
plays that required tables and chairs as part of their "realistic" content. In short, furniture—to our age perhaps
the most innocuous of all stage properties—was, as
Hartman would say, one of those "necessary and permitted profanation[s]" by which theater periodically
balances the tension between the pressing real world and
its own ritual.

I have chosen the relatively innocent advent of furniture on the stage as a symptom of a phenomenon we
might call preconventional shock: the alteration of the
"ceremony" by the intrusion of something with little
or no aesthetic history (I will qualify this in a moment).
By shock I mean nothing as dramatic as the shock produced by the great iconoclastic dramas (Hugo's *Hernani,* Ibsen's *Ghosts*): not shock as outrage but shock in
the sense that birth, or exposure, or discovery are
shocking; shock not only for the audience but for the
medium itself which has, as it were, stumbled onto
something with an unknown potential. Nor can we set
precise temporal limits on it; for shock of this sort
grows in sometimes imperceptible stages out of a gradually emerging "crisis" in the art, in Thomas Kuhn's
term, that demands "a reconstruction of the field from
new fundamentals, a reconstruction that changes some

of the field's most elementary theoretical generalizations as well as many of its paradigm methods and applications."[25] Most likely Montigny had no thought of revolutionizing the stage. We can assume that, like most directors with an instinct for the approaching cul-de-sac, he had simply wanted to do more interesting things with his materials. But once an image—especially a fundamental image like furniture—begins its life under new and open conditions, it begins to transform the possibilities of the art: it "transforms our vision," as Kuhn says, and in turn is itself transformed by our vision, if only in its struggle to escape degeneration into an empty sign. Things are first interesting because they are new; then (if they were not simply fads) because they fit into an order or help to create a new order; finally, they disappear into the order as one of the invisible building blocks out of which new images, and eventually new paradigms, are made. Above all, in the theater, as in any art, there is always the need to defamiliarize all of the old familiar defamiliarizations.

We could have approached the realistic paradigm from any number of directions or points in history; but in furniture we have perhaps its most concrete manifestation, for the whole phenomenology of realistic acting—especially as a reaction to classical acting—can be derived from it. If we reduce the realistic theater to its single most important property, we arrive, in effect, at the chair. Chairs, in some form, have probably been a staple property of the theater since Aristophanes; but

25. Thomas S. Kuhn, *The Structure of Scientific Revolutions* (Chicago: University of Chicago Press, 1970), p. 85.

we must make a distinction between the chair as an occasional necessity of stage action (the king on his throne, Hamlet sitting at court) and the chair as a collaborator in a new relationship between character and milieu. The modern actor knows the chair as one of the permanent tools of his art, primarily because it is the property that most directly engages his body in the stage world. For this reason the chair was as incidental to the placeless, timeless world of classical tragedy as it was indispensable to the salons and rooms of comedy (for example, the "table" scene in *Tartuffe*).

There is an appropriate remark in Bergson's *Laughter* that will make the idea clearer: "No sooner does anxiety about the body manifest itself than the intrusion of a comic element is to be feared. On this account, the hero in a tragedy does not eat or drink or warm himself. He does not even sit down any more than can be helped."[26] Bergson's remark takes us directly to the whole opposition of the "high" and the "low," the metaphysical and the social, on which drama's two master genres had more or less been kept apart since the ancient world. Why does the hero of tragedy not sit down "any more than can be helped"? Apart from the

26. Henri Bergson, *Laughter: An Essay on the Meaning of the Comic,* trans. Cloudesley Brereton and Fred Rothwell (New York: MacMillan, 1928), p. 52. In act 1 of Racine's *Phèdre,* for example, there is a rare stage direction, *Elle s'assit,* following Phèdre's line, "My eyes are dazzled to see the light again, / and my knees tremble and give way beneath me. / Alas!" This is scarcely a contradiction of the point Bergson is making. Rather, I would claim that it carries considerable shock value arising from its conspicuousness. Certainly the thought of Racine's characters typically lounging in chairs would be at comic odds with the extreme formality of his stage.

fact that it is hard to become tragic in the sitting position, there is the factor of anxiety about the body; there
is always a comic risk of the physical and the metaphysical spheres meeting head on, as would be the case were
Hamlet's chair to collapse while he pondered his destiny. Here I would treat anxiety about the body not as a
comic risk but as the behavioral ground from which realism springs: to sit is *to be,* to exist suddenly and plentifully in the material world ("I sit, therefore I am *here*");
and in this sense classical characters are bodiless: they
exist in a vague intersection between elsewheres established by poetry. But when characters begin to sit as
naturally as they stand, the body comes fully into its
own as the center of a new spatial concern, and this is
the sense in which realism and comedy are two faces of
the same coin. The proliferation of furniture on the
nineteenth-century stage was not simply a concession
to verisimilitude but a closure of comedy's social world
on the drama of high individualism. We may go even
further and add that with the chair we see the gradual
atrophy of verbal scenery: the stage picture ceases to be
a construct of language, an *anywhere* between elsewheres, and is now moored to a here and now in which
is lodged the very determinism of character and destiny. What the chair made possible, in a word, was conversation: casual or exploratory talk leading to tension
and crisis; the carving of the true subject out of the
seemingly phatic encounter ("Well, let's have that nice
little chat, Mrs. Tesman"). All told, speech ambling at
the speed of environment: tables, tea cups, fireplaces
and window views, the whole ensemble force of the
material world cast as the domain of status, the great

subject of the modern drama. But above all, the chair, *locus operandi* of the chat, the indispensable center without which the rest would be so much decoration. In the modern theater the chair (or such derivatives as Edward Albee's park bench and Beckett's urns) becomes: territorial preserve, weapon and shield (Ibsen and Pinter); the curse of the material world (Ionesco); the seat of anxiety, of time and place as enemy, of the problematical nature of existence among "the things" (Chekhov and Beckett). In sum, in the graphic economy of theater symbolism, rooms, like all images, must eventually justify their presence: they must inhabit the people who inhabit them.

Of course the realistic paradigm brings us no closer to the true phenomenological base of theater than any stylized paradigm. As in all arts this base rests finally in the immediacy of perception's encounter with a world. "Vision," Merleau-Ponty says, "is not a certain mode of thought or presence to self; it is the means given me for being absent from myself, for being present at the fission of Being from the inside—the fission at whose termination, and not before, I come back to myself."[27] Merleau-Ponty is speaking here of the art of painting. But is this not a perfect description of that lostness in the world of the play that we somewhat narrowly refer to as the willing suspension of disbelief? The actor takes us *into* a world within the world itself. At bottom, it is not a matter of the illusory, the mimetic, or the representational, but of a certain kind of *actual,* of having something before one's vision—and in the theater one's hearing—to which we join our being. The actor

27. Merleau-Ponty, *The Primacy of Perception,* p. 186.

enables us to recognize the human "from the inside": Olivier arouses *that* particular gesture in me; I am watching Olivier *exist* as Macbeth, and through this unique ontological confusion I exist myself in a new dimension. All this has much to do with signification and can be studied as such. But real engagement is an enhancement of being. What happens, *when* it happens, in the theater is, as Shakespeare's Polixenes might say, art. But the art itself is nature.

2

The Scenic Illusion: Shakespeare and Naturalism

The dramatist assigns his play to a scene, designated by language or by objects in space, without troubling to think how radically he has shifted the ground and conditions of our perception of the world. In a stroke he has altered our customary orientation to time and space. Consider the opening of any play. What we call the exposition is really the surreptitious planting of an embryo future in a reported past and the sealing off of time in an inevitable space. For a beginning, or a past, can only be posited from the vantage of a known future. It is what Paul Ricoeur calls the past absolute, an "unstable mixture of certainty and surprise" in which the past, freed from the infinite contingencies of reality, now corners the future and eliminates it as a category of care.[1] The curtain falls, or the lights dim, on a frozen moment in which living actors representing fictional beings become the finished figures of a sculptural group; or, to borrow a figure from Northrop Frye, something with a beginning and middle and end be-

1. Paul Ricoeur, *The Symbolism of Evil,* trans. Emerson Buchanan (Boston: Beacon Press, 1969), p. 221.

comes "a center and a periphery in mental space."[2] This is not achieved so much by a cessation of movement; the ubiquitous "freeze" of stage and film endings is only a symptom of the whole mysterious transformation of dramatic time into lyric space. Of course one could say that this is true of all fiction and of all so-called "time" arts; but it is the special province of the theater because the enacted play is the one art form, excepting the dance, that imitates human action in the medium, one might say, of human action. The actor is that unique creature who passes through a whole life in a few hours and in so doing carries the spectator vicariously with him. The term catharsis is too often reserved for tragedy, thanks to Aristotle, as if tragedy alone produced it by a unique process of the purging of two emotions that we understand so variously that one might say we don't understand them at all. The emotions generated by tragedy are probably more serious and transcendental than those generated by the more hybrid forms of drama. But putting this issue aside, catharsis is our best word for what takes place at large in the theater. It is precisely a purging: what is purged, at least on the level that concerns me here, is time—the menace of successiveness, of all life falling haphazardly through time into accident and repetition. The world at each instant, to paraphrase Nietzsche, is a successful solution of nature's own tensions.[3] To nature, in other

2. Northrop Frye, *A Natural Perspective: The Development of Shakespearean Comedy* (New York: Columbia University Press, 1965), p. 9.

3 Friedrich Nietzsche, *The Birth of Tragedy and the Genealogy of Morals,* trans. Francis Golffing (Garden City, N.Y.: Doubleday and Co., 1956), p. 9.

words, an automobile fatality is nothing but the successful solution to a certain tension in matter accumulating in a space we call Highway 101. A play is a successful, if temporary, refutation of this doctrine, whether it ends in death, marriage, or sheer continuance, as in much modern drama since Chekhov; that is, a play plucks human experience from time and offers an aesthetic completion to a process we know to be endless. The play imitates the timely in order to remove it from time, to give time a shape.

In this (and the following) chapter, however, I want to deal with stage space, the little room in which this purgative reckoning is made, because it seems natural to deal with space before dealing with what happens in it. Even this is a rather misleading justification since stage space and the stage event are one and the same thing; they are reciprocal entities, impossible to keep separate for very long, even for discussion purposes. There is even a level on which actors cannot be distinguished from furniture, since both are aspects of a composition in time and space. Designers and directors know this as artistic common sense, audiences as a vague impression of the stage as a kind of fluid painting. But for the present my project is to explore the sensory basis of scenic illusion. To this end it would be useful to posit two fundamental modes in which scenery is created and perceived: let us call them the *acoustical* and the *optical,* or the scenery that is heard and the scenery that is seen. From this strictly sensory, or affective, perspective we are thinking of scenery as our total impression of a play's world. We are not interested in scene design per se, as distinguished from other elements, but in seeing everything on the stage *scenically*: that is, as a shifting image in time and space, formed by the interplay of visual and aural events.

Let us begin with a passage from Merleau-Ponty's *Phenomenology of Perception* that will take us quickly to the phenomenal floor of scenic illusion, or at least to the manner in which the stage picture leads us by the senses into its world:

If I imagine a theatre with no audience in which the curtain rises upon illuminated scenery, I have the impression that the spectacle *is in itself visible* or ready to be seen, and that the light which probes the back and foreground, accentuating the shadows and permeating the scene through and through, in a way anticipates our vision. Conversely our own vision merely takes up on its own account and carries through the encompassing of the scene by those paths traced out for it by the lighting, just as, when we hear a sentence, we are surprised to discover the track of an alien thought. We perceive in conformity with the light, as we think in conformity with other people in verbal communication.[4]

Let us now suppose that the play has begun and that we have complicated the situation to the point that we have both light, playing against a scene, and speech. That is, we hear the tracks of alien thoughts in the words spoken by the characters and we see the scene before us traced out by the lighting. Immediately the scene will be upstaged by the speaking characters on whom our visual attention comes to rest. The stage will become a surrounding milieu, a peripheral crucible. Might we not now say that we perceive and think "in conformity with" a double stimulae—that, in a sense, we *hear* the

4. Merleau-Ponty, *Phenomenology of Perception,* p. 310.

scene and we *see* the speech? Or, that the speeches become a kind of metaphysical light cast on the setting,
while the illuminated setting encompasses the speech
and gives it a kind of environmental meaning (speech
spoken *only here*)? The scene "permeates" the speech
and the speech illuminates the setting. (We must not, of
course, ignore the contribution of the movement of actors and objects that assist immensely in this reciprocal
exchange.) What we discover from this fairly simple
sundering of elements is one of the phenomenal mys-
teries that makes theater so much more difficult to analyze than fiction, painting, or sculpture—theater being
in a sense a little of each.

In other words, as Merleau-Ponty says, "The senses
interact in perception as the two eyes collaborate in vision" (p. 234), or "The senses translate each other without need of an interpreter, and are mutually compre-
hensible without the intervention of any idea" (p. 235).
So a strange thing occurs: if one of the characters begins to talk about something taking place *elsewhere* in
his fictional world—at an office downtown, at the
beach, in a forest—the qualities established by this perceptual synthesis before us will vaguely infect this absent something that fills the mind's eye. For example,
when Anna, in Pinter's *Old Times,* speaks of the fact
that Kate and Deeley live on the seacoast, our image of
this sea and coastline "out there" is derived from the
drift of the dialogue, from the spareness of the room in
which she is speaking, from the absence or from the
presence, aural and visual, of all the details that have
accumulated in the closed linguistic and visual fields of
the play. The seacoast, in short, will be a qualitative extension of the setting.

So the ear sees scenery and the eye hears it. As a subsidiary text on this point it might be helpful to cite Rudolph Arnheim's distinction between pictorial and literary images: "A pictorial image presents itself whole, in simultaneity. A successful literary image grows through what one might call accretion by amendment. Each word, each statement, is amended by the next into something closer to the intended total meaning. This build-up through the stepwise change of the image animates the literary medium."[5] If anything, this distinction is too simple for the theater medium, which produces a combination of literary, pictorial, and even musical images constantly interpenetrating each other. It is true that dialogue works like the literary image in that it constantly "amends" its own images by accretion, as when you hear disease imagery in *Hamlet* so often that the whole world is finally infected, even when there is no disease imagery in the air. But language also amends the pictorial image of the setting. For example, the Greek stage remained substantially the same for all plays, apart from some emblematic paneling and machinery. But when the blind Oedipus came through the central portal of the *skene,* the audience "saw" a palace much different from the one it had perceived when these same doors opened to reveal, say, the corpses of Agamemnon and Cassandra in Aeschylus's earlier play. Even if nothing has changed scenographically, the play appropriates the stage as part of its qualitative world as established by its poetry. It is much the same process that an actor undergoes when Hamlet appropriates his body on one occasion and Macbeth on another.

5. Rudolf Arnheim, *Visual Thinking* (Berkeley and Los Angeles: University of California Press, 1969), pp. 249–50.

The idea of theater as a complex appeal to the senses seems the best axis on which to examine the phenomenal range of scenic illusion. It is obviously impossible to examine this range completely. But let us concentrate on three kinds of theater that may be said to round out the major possibilities of scenic illusion: the platform stage of Shakespeare, the realistic stage of Ibsen and Chekhov, and what I will simply call the postrealistic or experimental stage as we find it in the strain from Artaud and Brecht through Beckett and Grotowski. I choose these three loci, at the neglect of others (e.g., the spectacular operatic stage from the seventeenth-century forward, the symbolic Oriental stage, the medieval mansion stage), primarily because they are well-known, because all three are still available in our theater today, and because they present us with the clearest and most interesting shift in sensory appeal. Obviously, I will have to discuss them reductively—that is, in terms of their central illusionary principle: how what they characteristically do, differs. The first two I will deal with in the present chapter, the latter in the next, since modern experimentalism is so diverse in its forms.

There is probably no major theater in history, with the possible exception of Aeschylus's, that offers a purer instance of the powers of rhetorical scenery than the theater of Shakespeare. A great part of the language in Shakespeare is aimed at making us see "a kingdom for a stage," as the Chorus of *Henry V* puts it. In a sense, it was unnecessary for the Chorus to tell us this, since it is part of our bargain with any Shakespeare play that our "imaginary forces" piece out his "imperfections" in our thoughts. But the Chorus is less a plea to the audience to settle for imperfections than a hymn to the power of language to bridge the gulf between sign and thing. After all, a play that begins by asking us to

> Think, when we talk of horses that you see them
> Printing their proud hoofs i' th' receiving earth . . .
> *(Prologue, 26–27)*

has not so much apologized for the absence of horses as it has paraded them past us in the only form this theater requires. There is a good deal of this trickery in the Chrous and it has much in common with the trickery of Iago and Antony (in the forum speech) who, by eloquently naming the thing they would deny, print it all the more firmly on the mind. The fact is that naming— eloquently naming—anything constitutes the chief form of proof in this theater. It is by naming all the things no man could possibly do that Richard Crookback convinces us, and himself, that he is brilliant enough to do them:

> Can I do this, and cannot get a crown?
> Tut, were it farther off, I'll pluck it down.
> *(III, ii, 194–95)*

All of these instances are really only cameo imitations of Shakespeare's own larger trickery in exploiting the "imperfections" of his platform stage. Many of his allusions to this stage ("this unworthy scaffold") have about the edges of their seeming modesty a hint of au-

dacity at how much world can be crammed into so little room. Often this audacity reaches into his set
speeches and insets which seem to bask, like Richard,
in their own daring. A particularly good example is
Edgar's conjuration of the cliffs at Dover which, however functional otherwise, is an outrageous exercise in
inducing vertigo on a flat surface.[6]

I am suggesting that a certain tension between seeing
and hearing is a distinguishing feature of Shakespeare's
theater. It is the source of his virtuosity in the same
sense that the high wire is the source of the aerialist's
virtuosity. The very thickness of Shakespeare's world
is derived from the way in which poetry triumphs over
neutral space. This is not to say that the neutrality of
the Elizabethan platform stage is uninfluential as a visual phenomenon, or that there was no complementary
scenery on it. But its chief virtue was that it served as
a tabula rasa on which the actor could draw the ever-
shifting pictures of the text. This is one reason, among
several, that one often hears Shakespeare's world described as cinematic. It also explains why it is difficult
to remember, or even to know, where many scenes in
Shakespeare take place. Presumably, Laertes bids farewell to Ophelia somewhere in the Polonius household
(the Olivier film played it at the dock); but the imagery
conjures a scene of "nature crescent," outdoors among
the flowers in "the morn and liquid dew of youth."
Here, in fact, is an instance of how the characters of the
speakers are radiated into the environment. But the fact
that it doesn't matter where the scene takes place sug-

6. I explore the phenomenological possibilities of this speech in
"Standing on the Extreme Verge in *King Lear* and Other High
Places," *The Georgia Review* 36 (Summer 1982): 417–25.

gests how free the language is of the gravity of a palpable visual world. In a scene like this, and by extension in Shakespeare at large, the character creates a verbal world that bathes what we see before us in its quality. The stage becomes a kingdom held together by a physics of metaphorical attraction.

It is this peculiar physics that causes one of the critical problems of doing Shakespeare on film. When Shakespeare's cinematic language—able to carry us wherever the voice leads, "in motion of no less celerity than that of thought"—is grounded in the hard facts of a real world, caught by the camera's literal eye, we are apt to suffer a mild sensory confusion. If there is one way to make Shakespeare verbose, it is to speak his poetry in a milieu that usurps its descriptive function. There is no dawn that can do justice to Horatio's morn "in russet mantle clad," walking "o'er the dew of yon high eastward hill," because no dawn behaves in this way. Any attempt to imitate this imitation, or to supplement it with a more literal image of dawn breaking, will deprive the line of at least some of its unique sensory autonomy. It will make a poet out of Horatio, in the sense that language that seems relatively transparent on the stage tends to become artificial, or "poetic," when it is forced to compete with the urgent priorities of the eye. This is scarcely to say that Shakespeare and film are incompatible, but there is a subtle competition between the two modes of scene painting and it becomes most apparent when the camera tries to duplicate imagery that is itself serving a cinematic function. Two instances from recent films will illustrate. In Roman Polanski's *Macbeth,* an otherwise interesting film, Macbeth was led to Duncan's chamber by a glowing dagger superimposed on the staircase. Here, I suspect, it was a matter of giving the camera something metaphysical to look at during a long metaphysical speech. But the result was that one saw a real dagger rather than the chimerical one that Macbeth was seeing in his heat-oppressed brain. A more continuously disastrous instance occurs in the British TV production of *As You Like It*, which was shot on location in the environs of a Scottish castle. Here we are as far as imaginable from the Arden of the mind's eye or from Hawthorne's "poetic precinct where actualities will not be insisted upon." It is obviously possible for film to conjure romantic locales as effortlessly as poetry does (e.g., the Disney films), but the effect is compromised when the camera and the voice overlap, a little like two artists trying to paint the same landscape. Thus, when the Duke speaks of finding "sermons in stones and books in running brooks," the camera moved in for a close-up of a real brook, apparently in search of the ocular proof, and of course found only stones and water.

It is easy to be satirical about filmmakers who try to do Shakespeare, and I am far from denying that there are excellent films of the plays or that we aren't better off in having flawed films than none at all. The larger question here is: What happens when our two fundamental forms of scenery collide at the pitch of their unique powers? What happens when a dense metaphorical world collides with a dense real world (real, of course, only in the sense of the explicitness of photography)? Perhaps we could make more headway if we tied the problem strictly to theatrical presentation. Suppose we produce Shakespeare as we produce Ibsen. Suppose, in other words, that we clutter his stage world with furniture: tables, chairs, ornaments, paintings, carpets, candelabra, windows through which we see the fields, trees, and mountains of Renaissance perspective painting. Putting aside the productional impossibilities of rendering each scene in such detail, what would we have done to Shakespeare? In short, what happens when modern realism collides with renaissance romanticism?

Most obviously, we are involved here with still another kind of confusion in conventional realms. There are a number of reasons we would find such a mixture strange. Some of them would relate to our conventional expectations and habits in Shakespearean production, and it should be said that certain ages (the nineteenth century) strove for the equivalent of a realistic Shakespeare, and the results apparently delighted audiences at least some of the time. The rule we derive from this fact is of course that nothing is impossible, or contradictory, in theater if it satisfies a current enthusiasm. But in normative terms, what is phenomenally disjunctive in the hyper-realistic Shakespeare? If we can assume that in modern realistic drama there is a symbiotic relationship between scenery and language, then we can probably assume the same is true in Shakespeare's theater. This is not to argue that there is a best way of doing Shakespeare or even, categorically, a wrong way, but that when we tamper with his word/scene ratio—to adapt a Kenneth Burke term to my own uses—we are apt to experience the sort of phenomenal strangeness I have been trying to define here.

If we were to ask why there is no furniture, or very little, on Shakespeare's stage—bypassing the obvious historical and conventional explanations and thus attempting to interpret the logic of the conventions themselves—we would have to conclude that it would serve no purpose because the play does not require, or even acknowledge, its existence. The world of objects is neither problematical nor influential; or to be more accurate, it is only *selectively* influential, as when Hamlet uses the player's recorder to warn Rosencrantz and Guildenstern that he cannot be played upon, or when Macduff pulls his hat about his ears on hearing of the death of his family. In this connection it is interesting to note how little attention Shakespeare's people pay to their given environment; there is, in other words, very little reference, gestural or vocal, to the practical furnishings of the world through which they move. Objects are of little interest to them; or when they become interesting, as the recorder and the skull do to Hamlet, or the joint stool to Lear, the character invariably sees through the thing itself, via a metaphor, leaving it, so to speak, with one foot in reality and the other in some vaster symbolic realm. Such metaphorical conversions also take place in the realistic drama, where glass animals and wild ducks do double duty as symbols; the key difference is that in Shakespeare the symbol is almost always constructed from words. Skulls are more often heard than seen and hang in the air only so long as the character is tracking larger things—the convenience of this stage being that when something is out of mind it is also out of sight.

This is probably as good a ground as any on which to contrast Shakespeare's theater with the representational theater that gradually displaced the platform stage over the ensuing centuries. I will center on the high, or mature, phase of this evolution as best exampled in the theater of Ibsen and Chekhov, which contains almost everything about representational theater that is either interesting or unique. Obviously metaphor collapses in this theater, at least as a native form of speech. This has less to do with the idea that people in real rooms must speak realistically than with the fact that metaphor—as we find it in Shakespeare at least—is a tropical strategy for abridging the very powers of the solid-state world from which realism was to draw its peculiar gravity. Like the science that inspired it, realism was essentially an art of pinning things down. The stage served as a kind of laboratory where heretofore unarticulated social processes and species could be examined under the strong light of the new electrical lamp. The object of the realistic setting was not only to look like a real room but to collaborate in a new relationship between perceived space and heard language. A sociological examination of this relationship would lead us to some variation of the naturalistic code expressed best by Zola: "Instead of abstract man I would make a natural man, put him in his proper surroundings, and analyze all the physical and social causes which make him what he is."[7] Phenomenologically, our interest would lie on a different tangent. We would want to know how this environment (such a "surrounding") expressed itself as an affective influence that carried the underlying principles of realism to its audience; that is to say, how metaphor was displaced by another referential system by which big things could be crammed into small places.

7. Emile Zola, "Naturalism on the Stage," in *The Experimental Novel and Other Essays,* trans. Belle M. Sherman (New York: Haskell House, 1964), p. 151.

We have an almost perfect example of what realism put in the place of metaphor when Hedda Gabler sweeps on stage in the opening scene of Ibsen's play and says, "Good heavens—what a nuisance! That maid's opened the window and let in a whole flood of sunshine!" The closest thing to poetry here is the dead metaphor "flood of sunshine," a far cry from Horatio's "morn in russet mantle clad." The quality of the line, however, is not to be found in its style or in its homeliness but in its fusion of "pictorial" and "literary" imagery. The line implies a speaker who is *in* her world in a certain way; she is, in fact, imbedded in it, surrounded by actuality. One might say that the speech is centripetal, the product of a world in which speech is conditioned by the persistence of environment and the passing of clock time. To predicate an immediate outside, with a rising sun, is to posit what we might call a Ptolemaic universe—that is, a world whose center is *here*, will remain here, and the elsewhere will revolve obediently around it. A line like this, or one put to this use, would be out of place in Shakespeare if only because windows do not really exist until called into being by the emerging circumstances of the plot. *Romeo and Juliet* suddenly requires a window in act 2 ("But soft! What light through yonder window breaks?"), but it is only the frame for an elaborate Copernican metaphor ("It is the east, and Juliet is the sun"). In other words, windows, like skulls and joint stools, are there to be seen through, not to be the occasion for conspiratorial symbolism. It is obvious that any object in Shakespeare can serve as a symbol, roughly in Ibsen's sense; but this has nothing to do with the encroachment of environment on character. The Shakespeare character creates nature for his own (and the play's) immediate use; he hauls it, out of thin air, into brief service as a hyperbolic extension of his emotion; for example, Lear, lamenting Cordelia's death, observes that dogs, horses, and rats continue, alas, to live, but poor perdu is lost. So much for the animal kingdom.

We can draw this comparison into a larger context by taking a characteristic example of spoken landscape from modern drama. In Astrov's monologue on the forests in *Uncle Vanya,* much too long to quote here, there is probably more raw nature (animals, trees, swamps, country-side) than we typically get in one chunk in Shakespeare; so one could hardly say that Chekhov has no use for the visual world beyond his stage. But the speech is not a means of incorporating this world into his play for its own sake, or of using nature as an indispensable part of speech to serve the emotional needs of the play. It is the-matically relevant: its content, in fact, is the destruction of nature by human ignorance, a theme that runs through the drama from Ibsen to the American realists. Nature is what man has not got, and it usually gets into the play by way of nostalgia. Even in O'Neill (for exam-ple, *Desire Under the Elms*) living in nature is problemati-cal at best. A character like Ephram Cabot can conjure sermons in stones, but he cannot live in sympathy with the land without severe hardship. In fact, this hardship and ways to endure it is exactly the underlying subject of the play. One somehow expects any serious modern play set in nature to be a chronicle of lost or rapidly dis-appearing values. It is hard, in contrast, to imagine a Shakespeare character looking into the evening sky and remarking how "purty" it is, not because Shakespeare's people don't appreciate sunsets but because the distinction between environment and men living in it has not yet become a dramatic theme. Hamlet may talk nostalgically of the majestical roof fretted with golden fire, but his is an unusual case of nostalgia brought on more by private isolation than by a change in celestial landscape. The point is that when nature is the subject of poetry in Shakespeare, it is not perceived as threatening or beautiful in itself but as a mirror image of what is threatening or beautiful in a single soul or in the body social. Nature's revolt is always a moral revolt, and when the time is free everything returns to its normal state, at which point it becomes a benign garden that might serve as the locale for another play when time, once again, reveals the serpent under the flowers. One thinks offhand of the gillyflower passages in *The Winter's Tale,* where flowers become the cause of a debate on just where one can draw the line between nature and art. The convincing idea that there is no art but that art which nature makes is inconceivable in a world where nature and human consciousness lie in two different realms.

To return to the Ibsen passage, what is more importantly occurring in Hedda's line is the inevitable bonding of scenery and character, environment and psychology. The here and now of realism, at least in its psychological phase, is finally a medium for externalizing an interior—in this case, a woman's whole hostility toward her marriage and her life. It is important to note that the interior is not thereby defined, as it would be in Shakespearean soliloquy. We get only the sign, or product, of a motive, not the motive itself. The line puts us on notice that there is more here than meets the eye or the ear. Ibsen would not have been able to draw Hedda out without the successive parade of objects (windows, flowers, slippers, photo albums, hats, and dueling pistols) that constitute her moorings in the given world.

Perhaps the point can be summed up if we apply a well-known idea from Roman Jacobson.[8] We might say that the loss of metaphor led to the discovery of metonymy (or, if you wish, synecdoche, since one figure is as prominent as the other in realistic theater). For what the drama, of all the arts, requires is a way of allowing the stage to contain things outside of it and to make visible things that are invisible. Metaphor is a device for getting in more world on the principle of similarity, or correspondence, whereby the world imitates the action, as when "the very stones" prate of Macbeth's whereabouts, or Laertes compares his sister's virtue to the "infant" flowers of the spring. Metonymy and synecdoche, as we find them on the realistic stage, are devices for reducing states, or qualities, or attributes, or whole entities like societies, to visible things in which they somehow inhere. Of course, the novel had perfected these tropes long before the drama got around to using them seriously. Only with the emergence of psychological realism in the drama—a good date is Zola's dramatization of his novel *Thérèse Raquin* in 1873—did it become apparent that the furniture and paraphernalia that were still, for the most part, painted on the canvas flats could be moved into the setting and charged with psychological or metaphysical energy. One could, as Hamlet put it, find a quarrel in a straw, or in a window, a principle that

8. Roman Jakobson and Morris Halle, "The Metaphoric and Metonymic Poles," in *Fundamentals of Language* ('s-Gravenhage: Mouton, 1956), pp. 76–82. See also: Roman Jakobson, "Linguistics and Poetics," in *Style in Language,* ed. Thomas A. Sebeok (Cambridge: MIT Press, 1960), pp. 355–77.

Pinter carries to the extreme in plays like *The Caretaker* and *The Homecoming*. In a sense, Pinter's characters are the offspring of Hedda Gabler in that they are forever waging war with things and speaking provocative lines reminiscent of Hedda's ("Who ate my cheese-roll?" or "You're sitting in my chair!").

There is a still larger aspect of this shift from metaphor to metonymy. The characteristic setting of the realistic drama is the living room. In one respect, it was the outcome of realism's greatest limitation, its commitment to a particular scene that could not be changed without interruption and further expense. But as the most versatile intersection of the private and social spheres, the living room was the predictable destination of realism insofar as realism was an attempt to put the human drama into the visible real world of everyday social interaction and to reveal, above all else, how that world was the primary causal factor in experience. Like all realistic locales, the living room is invariably a conditioning environment and all things that pass in it do so by virtue of the limitations it implies. Formally, these are the limitations of time, place, and action, whereby realism, while trying to imitate reality faithfully, became a kind of unintentional neoclassicism. Thematically, they are roughly the limitations of the inhabitants' own history of birth, choice, and class made visible in what we might call a moment of space. As Hamlet might say, it has all come to this; and stage directions in realistic plays amount to a careful sprinkling of artifacts that look in opposite directions. Like General Gabler's pistols, they are both the relics of a causal past and omens of things to come. Taken together, they form a sort of infra-plot through which the action passes and defines itself, as in those coloring-book pictures children make by drawing lines through a series of numbers. Thus, with the increasing specificity of stage directions in modern plays ("Walks to table; picks up newspaper," etc.), one is usually watching the encroachment of a symbol-laden space on a private psychology. As Burke says, the stage setting contains the action ambiguously.[9] One might say that the characters explicate the setting in their dialogue as one explicates a painting—at the same time, of course, the setting is explicating character pictorially, much as a prison cell may be said to explicate a conversation taking place within it. For example, Hedda's progress through the areas and objects of her living room, from her entrance to the sofa, to the fireplace, to the pistol case, to the inner room where she finally takes her life, is a progress much like that of the medieval drama through the successive mansions, or stations, between Creation and Judgment. All of these "stations" are visible from the beginning, nestling casually in their innocent verisimilitude, but their contribution becomes evident only as they are folded into the action. For example, the Maid's line in act 2, "Shall I make up the fire, ma'am?" is a characteristic instance of Ibsen's causal masquerading as the casual. Such a line would be foreign in Shakespeare because, as a plant for the big event of the next act, it presupposes a world in which one event sets up another within a tight system of time-space probabilities. There is no "leaping o'er times" when the center of the dramatic universe is a room of

9. Kenneth Burke, *A Grammar of Motives and A Rhetoric of Motives* (Cleveland: World Publishing Co., 1962), p. 3.

solidly signifying objects, each one waiting its turn to become purposeful. And though, as Hedda burns Lovborg's manuscript, one does not consciously think, "*Now* I see why there is a fire!" there is a subliminal wonder in the self-sufficiency of the room to have contained, in advance, all of the properties necessary to produce this unique reckoning in time.

This confinement of the action to a single loaded locale, or at most two or three, is one of the realistic theater's greatest affective advantages—or, to put it a better way, it is the limitation on which it capitalized most successfully. The fact that everything is in view, lying in wait, gives the stage a great deal of its optical and temporal interest. This quality of still silent participation is one that not even the film, a medium exceptionally hospitable to realistic representation, can duplicate. For the very mobility of the camera eye, even when it remains in the room, counteracts the power of a rigid omnipresent space that gradually surrenders its randomness and becomes the inevitable container of a human event. We can almost always recognize a film that has been based on a play, especially one from the Ibsen tradition, by the stubborn inwardness in the proceedings that survives the translation. The characters insist on talking about things, as opposed to doing things in the open world. Their actions are aftermaths: we meet them, as it were, at the point where their lives turn into conversations. As a result, the camera, unable to bear too much sameness, becomes restless; like a child, it longs to be outdoors and usually (in films like *The Caretaker, The Homecoming, Long Day's Journey into Night,* and *Who's Afraid of Virginia Woolf?*) manages to sneak there, to find windows, one might say, in the tight walls of the stage script. What is sacrificed, for certain gains of course, is the tension between the theatrically given, or allowable, space and the destinies to be worked out in it. Part of the wonder of a good realistic play is how skillfully it manages to charge such a small space with so much energy. We know that human dramas do not unfold in one or two rooms. But when a play seduces us into believing that they do—that is, when the smoothness in the flow of events overtakes the artifice of the form—we have the spatial counterpart of the radical improbability that Fate performs in the temporal action. Space is destiny, the visual proof that order lurks in human affairs. In short, what the realistic theater accomplishes, subliminally, is the imprisonment of the eye. Strindberg summed it up in one phrase: "The impact of the *recurring* milieu."[10] Thus, one of the two senses through which theater comes to us is locked into a hypnotic sameness, while the other, the ear, hears of developments and changes in affairs that seem to offer a degree of choice and freedom in the lives of the characters. The dialogue says, in effect, "We are here only temporarily. We are free to go elsewhere"; the setting says, in effect, "It will all end here!" For example, at the end of *Long Day's Journey into Night*, a play in which this impression of spatial fatality is extremely

10. August Strindberg, "On Modern Drama and Modern Theatre," in *Playwrights on Playwriting: The Meaning and Making of Modern Drama from Ibsen to Ionesco*, ed. Toby Cole (New York: Hill and Wang, 1963), p. 16. In this same volume see also Arthur Miller's view of the failure of the film version of *Death of a Salesman*. For example: "I believe that the basic reason—aside from the gross insensitivity permeating its film production—was that the dramatic tension of Willy's memories was destroyed by transferring him, lit-

strong, the Tyrones are grouped in silence around the table as Mary retreats into the narcotic dreamworld where she had been happy "for a time." What we see, essentially, is an action finally coming to rest in the rigid space prepared for it in advance; it is as if the walls, the chairs, and the tables, like the Moira, knew all along that it could not have been otherwise.

This idea of the fateful participation of the setting in the drama is not much of a factor in pleasant realism or in realistic comedy, where the stage is often little more than a backdrop illustrating a certain social status or a benign obstacle course of misbehaving props and unreliable hiding places. But it comes to a grim and subtle perfection in the plays of Chekhov, whom we like to think of as a comedian. And before moving on to the final phase of scenic illusion I will deal with here, I

---

erally, to the locales he had only imagined in the play. There is an inevitable horror in the spectacle of a man losing consciousness of his immediate surroundings to the point where he engages in conversations with unseen persons. The horror is lost—and drama becomes narrative—when the context actually becomes his imagined world. And the drama evaporates because psychological truth has been amended, a truth which depends not only on what images we recall but in what connections and contexts we recall them. The setting on the stage was never shifted, despite the many changes in locale, for the precise reason that, quite simply, the mere fact that a man forgets where he is does not mean that he has really moved. Indeed, his terror springs from his never-lost awareness of time and place" (p. 264).

would like to look more closely at his stage, primarily because in his living rooms we detect the emergence of a characteristic modern attitude that makes him an almost ideal transition to the postrealistic stage.

Let us begin by trying to imagine Chekhov's play on a bare platform stage. Can we imagine his characters looking through windows that aren't there, addressing bookcases of the mind, moving through the invisible detritus of a dying civilization? More specifically, what exactly would happen to the play without its furniture? My guess is that the space could be filled by our imagination, in much the same way that we fill Thornton Wilder's empty spaces on slight verbal and mimic cues —were it not for another factor. It is the time scheme that would be out of joint. In Chekhov, furniture is visible history: the predicament of life—its "persistent low-keyed unpleasure," in David Reisman's phrase—is lodged in furniture.

Chekhov's plays might be called epics of claustrophobia, in the sense that he often called for three or four changes of setting in a single play (a tendency he may have inherited from other Russians who were, on the whole, rather cavalier about scenery). The fact is, with a few adjustments his plays could have been confined to one setting, unlike Ibsen's, since nothing much is said in one room that could not have been said in another. So there is very little pragmatic or dramaturgic reason behind such shifts. The real logic has to do with atmosphere: for the movement from room to room of the same house, or from the interior to the outside, is a merciless commentary on human possibilities. *Plus ça change:* Chekhov's people remain the same no matter where they are. This has to do, in part, with what they talk about. When they sit down to talk, as they usually do, about life elsewhere, or two hundred years hence, or about the need to work, furniture becomes the seat of discontent; to be in one world and to dream of another is to confer on one's living space the status of a prison. But it has to do more deeply with the very pace and rhythm of life. To imagine a Chekhov character bustling through his rooms toward some less immediate goal than a birthday party is to redefine the space in terms of utility. Very often, his characters are already sitting as the play opens. That is, we pick up their lives in a continuing past tense. Nothing puts the play so securely in the realm of endurance as this "discovered" tableau. It is not that time is being passed. Time is an old condition, like rheumatism or arthritis, that one tolerates. It is not, strictly speaking, boredom, but an accommodation to boredom. Boredom becomes an *activity* in Chekhov, a little like that of Mann's tuberculars on the magic mountain who spend what is left of their lives "reading" their X rays. Indeed, time accompanies the Chekhov character like the odor of a disease. It is his inescapable medium and it rubs off on the walls and furnishings which *are,* like the people, by virtue of *having been.* As the old Russian proverb goes: "That which was, is. That which is, will be." Time gives itself away in Chekhov as space gives itself away in Ibsen (the pistols are waiting over there; the inner room frames the watchful eye of General Gabler; Hedda always enters from up left). There are no such strategic locations in Chekhov's rooms because there is very little on stage that holds a hidden meaning. The Chekhov room is a communal locale, not a gridwork of defensive and offensive domains. It is shared space: visitors move in it as if they had always been there. In fact, you can't tell the visitors from the residents.

As a result, the Chekhov character sits in his chair differently from the Ibsen character, who always seems to sit on the edge of it, bursting with news or curiosity. In Ibsen a chair is a chair, until one decides to use it as a weapon (Engstrand cannily refusing to sit with his betters, Hedda sitting between Thea Elvsted and Lovborg); but for the most part one sits down in Ibsen to have a leading conversation, for only from chairs can the intricacies of motive be unraveled. In Chekhov, however, the chair is the evidence of the Chekhov habit. The world of objects is a slumbering cat; it has no purpose but to serve as the still point against which we observe a dreadful passage of soul. Osip Mandelstam made a perceptive remark about Chekhov in complaining about the Moscow Art Theatre's "distrust of the word." The famous pauses in its productions of Chekhov, he said, "are nothing other than a holiday of pure tactile sensation. Everything grows quiet, and only a silent tactile sensation remains" in which the audience "touches" the furniture with its eyes.[11] This is exactly right: what happens in a Chekhov silence is that the tactile world, the visible world (which the talk is aimed unconsciously at keeping at bay), this history-in-objects, quietly encroaches on the human, like the creeping vegetation in Sartre's Bouville. Suddenly, you can hear the ticking of the objects and the ceaseless flow of future into past: the world is no longer covered by conversation.

11. Osip Mandelstam, *The Complete Critical Prose and Letters*, trans. Jane Gary Harris and Constance Link (Ann Arbor, Mich.: Ardis, 1979), p. 189. I wish to thank Ephim Fogel at Cornell University for calling this essay to my attention.

How different this silence is from silence in Ibsen, which bristles with attentiveness and expectation, with thinking. Out of Ibsen will come Pinter; out of Chekhov, Beckett. In other words, if stage conversation is filled with inuendo, with subterfuge, with the charge of intrigue, silence—when it falls—will emit these same energies. Silence is the same warfare by other means. But when stage conversation is filled with emptiness, as it is in Chekhov, or with a form of emotion and anguish that has no specific derivation and no promise of surcease through possibilities in the world of action, silence—when it falls—will be the "negative equivalent" of this emptiness.[12]

The reader may find this view of Chekhov unnecessarily dark. I have tried to draw out—perhaps I should say to exaggerate—this peculiar tension between word and scene, figure and ground, because it offers us a foundation, in thoroughly naturalistic terms, for an approach to the postrealistic word/scene relationship. Some years ago, I wrote an essay on Chekhov that was to some extent a gloss on Frye's idea that in Chekhov's plays, or in certain parts of them, "we are coming about as close to pure irony as the stage can get." By irony, or the ironic attitude, Frye here refers to the emergence in the nineteenth century of a kind of play in which "the sense of inevitable event begins to fade out, and the sources of catastrophe come into view." The ironic play is a fusion of comic detachment and tragic subjectivity,

12. Gisele Brelet, "Music and Silence," in *Reflections on Art: A Source Book of Writings by Artists, Critics, and Philosophers,* ed. Susanne K. Langer (New York: Oxford University Press, 1961), p. 111.

the study of "the combined pressure of a reactionary society without and a disorganized soul within."[13]

In terms of scenic illusion it seems to me that this attitude inevitably implies a putting at odds of action and world, the human figure and the scenic ground, the visual and the aural. If metonymy and synecdoche are means of reducing and transporting whole worlds by substituting parts for wholes, or parts for the qualities of wholes, irony is a means of expanding our perspective beyond the part-whole entity. One could say that scenery, like anything else, is ironic when it negates what is being said in it, as when people in a prison cell talk about freedom; this is perhaps what Duerrenmatt meant by "turning the word against the scene."[14] But irony is, in our present concern at least, not so much a trope in itself as a disease that other tropes get. In *Metahistory* Hayden White suggests that irony is "metatropological"; that is, it "points to the potential foolishness of all linguistic characterizations of reality as much as to the absurdity of the beliefs it parodies."[15] Metaphor, metonymy, and synecdoche are thus "naive" tropes in the sense that their use implies belief in "language's capacity to grasp the nature of things in figurative terms" (pp. 36–37). Irony is a "hovering" trope, as

13. Northrop Frye, *Anatomy of Criticism* (Princeton, N.J.: Princeton University Press, 1957), p. 285.

14. Friedrich Duerrenmatt, "Problems of the Theatre," *Tulane Drama Review* 3 (1958): 11. I must add that Duerrenmatt is discussing this principle as it applies to his play *The Blind Man*.

15. Hayden White, *Metahistory: The Historical Imagination in Nineteenth-Century Europe* (Baltimore: Johns Hopkins University Press, 1975), p. 37.

Kierkegaard would want to add, and when it attaches itself to a metaphor or a metonymy or a synecdoche it infects it, one might say, with self-skepticism. For irony, White continues, is also "transideological" in the sense that, "as the basis of a world view, [it] tends to dissolve all belief in the possibility of positive political action" (p. 38).

In Ibsen we reach the epitome of the nineteenth-century realistic theater's faith in tropological discourse. Obviously Ibsen is steeped in irony of all kinds, but his figural and symbolic apparatus is substantially "naive," in White's sense (and in no other), because it is the servant of one of the most intense of ethical imaginations. Ibsen may be ironical at times about the myopic way some of his characters interpret their private symbols (a wild duck, a steeple, an orphanage), but overall Ibsen confidently constructs a world of ethical meanings—an ideology (whose precise tenets, of course, we may debate)—out of the building blocks of metonymy and synecdoche. We usually know what Ibsen is *for* and *against*. Even without the benefit of his notes we know what he thought about George Tesman's painstaking research on industry in Brabant as against Lovborg's shocking history of the future. Tesman lives *on* his work, Ibsen writes in his notes, Lovborg lives *for* his work. The scenic translation of this work dialectic was, for Ibsen, a matter of finding the proper metonymic *gestus,* as Brecht would say; and it is eventually communicated to us unmistakably (among other means) in the piles of books Tesman carries on stage which stand in sharp contrast to the jottings stuffed carelessly into Lovborg's jacket pockets.

In Chekhov we arrive at the moment when realism can no longer render the true content of its perceived reality ("life as it is") with its traditional system of tropes and symbols. It is not that the tropes and symbols fall into disuse, and it is not that vast entities, such as life in Czarist Russia, cannot be summed up in an image like the cherry orchard. But it is hard to find the bottom line of the signification because whatever the meaning is, it is subethical. The tropes have somehow got skewed, or ironized: the ethical foundation of realism—its "underlying moral fervor," in Victor Brombert's term[16]—has given way to a skepticism, not toward ideologies but toward the possibilities of existence itself, and one has the sense of a hovering author who is as diabolically equivocal—if not plain diabolical—as his people are gentle. The decline in theatricality (plot, action, intrigue) that so impressed and confused us in Chekhov's plays derives specifically from a more or less sudden absence of argument and discussion as the primary source of dramatic energy. Some of Chekhov's people argue endlessly (Tusenbach and Vershinin, for example) and it is quite possible to see that Chekhov is saying something himself—that he is *against* "dreaming" and *for* "work"—but one would hardly argue that his plays were written as proofs of such ideas or that Chekhov's self-imposed mission was to hold a mirror up to Russian character. It would be more in order to say that the plays use these tendencies as carriers of something else, in somewhat the way that

16. Victor Brombert, *The Romantic Prison: The French Tradition* (Princeton, N.J.: Princeton University Press, 1978), p. 57.

Shakespeare uses the tendency of murder as a carrier in *Macbeth*. Making Chekhov into any sort of polemicist is like locating the meaning of *Macbeth* in the premise that crime does not pay. The true dialectic in Chekhov occurs not between voices but between the single voice of the "disorganized soul" and the "reactionary" echo of silence in reality.

The point can be summed up in one example. When Gaev addresses the bookcase in *The Cherry Orchard,* he is, one might say, addressing it as a metonymy or synecdoche for the cultured past on this estate: "Dear honoured bookcase! Hail to thee who for more than a hundred years hast served the pure ideals of good and justice." And indeed, he is right, in a sense: the bookcase is a remnant of Gaev's world, as he remembers it. "Naive" realism would put such a bookcase on stage for just such a symbolic purpose; or it might do so to illustrate pedantry, or learning, or anything else that might be derived from the symbolism of books. In Ibsen it would be planted early on and wait for its moment in the play; in Shaw we might even be told the titles of the books on the shelves. On Chekhov's stage the bookcase is only negligibly symbolic in this sense; it might just as well have been a portrait, a grandfather clock, or a samovar. Like everything in Chekhov's rooms, like the rooms themselves, it has one master function: to constitute the ironic nonresponse of the world. We laugh at Gaev's speech, sad as it may be, for the same reason that we laugh on overhearing someone talking to an object. The bookcase does not hear Gaev. Yet it is a commentary on his speech, a visual metatext to the spoken text, and it is saying virtually what Proust says about Combray:

The reality that I had known no longer existed. . . . The places that we have known belong now only to the little world of space on which we map them for our own convenience. None of them was ever more than a thin slice, held between the contiguous impressions that composed our life at that time; remembrance of a particular form is but regret for a particular moment; and houses, roads, avenues are as fugitive, alas, as the years.[17]

17. Marcel Proust, *Swann's Way,* trans. C. K. Scott Moncrieff (New York: Modern Library, 1956), p. 611.

3

The Scenic Illusion: Expressionism and After

Two major threads of modernism come together in the almost seamless fabric of Chekhov's plays. We can look at Chekhov through two different lenses. We can see his plays as a demonstration of how far the descriptive function of realism could be carried, how close art could come to the rhythm of "life as it is" (his own phrase). Plays have gotten even more eventless since Chekhov, but no twentieth-century dramatist has managed to lift the representation of casual behavior to such a high level of art. But Chekhov cannot be circumscribed in the terms realism and naturalism. We can also see a lyrical, or impressionistic, or Maeterlinckian side of Chekhov. Here we bear on the famous Chekhov mood, *nastroenie,* which has brought as many Chekhov productions to grief as the naturalism. It is not that there are two discrete sides of Chekhov, for the impressionism is, in one sense, only a refinement of the naturalism. Georg Lukács remarks that in Maeterlinck the naturalistic techniques arrive at complete abstraction.[1] To develop the idea further: if you press the con-

1. Georg Lukács, *Writer and Critic and Other Essays,* ed. and trans. Arthur D. Kahn (New York: Grosset and Dunlap), p. 171.

creteness of the here and now far enough, you arrive at the infrastructure of reality, or the laws that hold reality up. There is a point where scrupulous attention to detail—for example, a photo of the pores of the skin— leads one back, or out, to the universe of geometric mass. In terms of human behavior, concentration on nuance, on the universe of microaction, leads, in the hands of the right artist, to general statements about "condition." Such a play is perhaps best described in Frye's term, *archetypal masque,* which "takes place in a world of human types, which at its most concentrated becomes the interior of the human mind."[2] I am thinking particularly of the strain of impressionistic plays from Maeterlinck to Beckett where the characters seem to be enacting a drama of pure consciousness under a naturalistic shell of language. For example, this passage from Maeterlinck's *The Intruder:*

THE UNCLE: What shall we do while we are waiting?

THE GRANDFATHER: Waiting for what?

THE UNCLE: Waiting for our sister.

THE FATHER: You see nothing coming, Ursula?

THE ELDEST DAUGHTER: *(At the window)* No, father.

THE FATHER: And in the avenue?—You see the avenue?

THE DAUGHTER: Yes, father; it is moonlight, and I see the avenue as far as the cypress wood.

THE GRANDFATHER: And you see no one, Ursula?

THE DAUGHTER: No one, grandfather.[3]

The similarity to Beckett here goes deeper than the static situation and the verbal images that recur in *Wait-*

2. Frye, *Anatomy of Criticism,* p. 291.

3. Maurice Maeterlinck, *The Plays of Maurice Maeterlinck,* trans. Richard Hovey (New York: Herbert S. Stone, 1972), p. 220.

ing for Godot and *Endgame*. Here we see the peculiar co-
operation of text and metatext so common in impressionism. Apart from the slight stiltedness, we hear the
pace and detail of real speech, speech concerned with a
real out there; but we also have the feeling that speech is
referring to another landscape that can be seen only
with the metaphysical eye. Nothing is, in fact, but what
is not. Chekhov, who greatly admired Maeterlinck's
"strange, wonderful" plays,[4] wrote a little drama of
pure consciousness himself and put it into *The Sea Gull*
where he made fun of it, or at least his characters did;
but it is actually a signature if not a self-parody, of what
he was doing in his plays in naturalistic disguise. If you
squint out the paraphernalia of random reality in Chekhov and think of his people as a kind of collective consciousness, you are left with a monologue of the soul
much like that in Treplev's playlet: "I am alone . . . , I
open my lips to speak, and in this void my sad echo is
unheard." Of course Chekhov would never allow his
own characters to say anything so pathetic, but the essence of this emotional subtext pervades his work to
the breaking string of *The Cherry Orchard,* where he is
flirting openly with what was later called surrealism.

When drama arrives at the point where it is about people who dream, rather than act, it is on the verge of giving birth to the dream play, or to the drama of the interior of the human mind. (I am putting aside the obvious
example of Strindberg here because his is such a clear
case of a dramatist who broke with one form [natura-

4. Anton Chekhov, *Letters on the Short Story, the Drama, and Other
Literary Topics,* ed. Louis S. Friedland (New York: Benjamin Blom,
1964), p. 264.

lism] and moved, more or less wholesale, to another [surrealism].) The best treatment of this journey to the interior has been written by Raymond Williams, who argues that the "break" between naturalism and the various nonrealisms that succeeded it must be seen not in "the look of the stage" but as the steady evolution of a "structure of feeling" based on "a passion for truth, in strictly human and contemporary terms." Thus broadly conceived, the naturalist drama is "one of the great revolutions in human consciousness: to confront the human drama in its immediate setting, without reference to 'outside' forces and powers."[5] There is always, he says, "a precise internal relation" between a structure of feeling and its set of stylistic conventions, and the naturalist drive toward its constantly evolving truth often found it necessary to slough off conventions because they were no longer true enough—all of which gave the product the look of a new "ism." Being a sort of scientist, the naturalist found himself in the position of the physicist searching for the elementary particle: every time he thought he had found it, a still more elementary particle signaled its existence. Or, today's truth is tomorrow's received idea; today's realism is tomorrow's melodrama. Thus naturalism moved increasingly inward to subtler and more subjective kinds of experience, creating its own conventions or borrowing them from earlier forms as it advanced. To abbreviate a complex metamorphosis: once realism had perfected the fusion of psychology and scenery—finding, as it were, the mind's construction in the environment—the next step was immanent. The

5. Raymond Williams, *The Drama from Ibsen to Brecht* (New York: Oxford University Press, 1969), p. 334.

clearest moment of conventional transformation, or at least the most important for the theater, is expressionism, which, Williams says, is realism turned inside out. Once you have trapped your protagonist in one of these *real* rooms, leaving him (or her) in the posture of Munch's creature in *The Cry*, you take away the room—which is no longer *real* enough—and reconstruct it as the visible extension of his ravaged state of mind. For example, as the story of a woman who dreams of living dangerously, imagine an expressionistic *Hedda Gabler* that takes place in the barrel of a dueling pistol; or a *Cherry Orchard* set among trees that gradually turn into telegraph poles and industrial smokestacks.

The refreshing thing about Williams's approach is that it enables us to see an evolution as a continual process rather than as something that began and ended as a manifestation of style. However distinctive the look of the expressionistic stage, it was doing the work of the naturalist premise either in its pessimistic aspect (with respect to society's victimization of the individual) or in its essentialist aspect (with respect to its intense concern for the state of the soul). Above all, it was still representational in the sense that it sought to depict faithfully its experience "in human and contemporary terms." The distinctive thing about the naturalists and the expressionists was that theirs was an art of fierce signification—meaning that if the play was interesting, if the audience drew its breath in outrage or astonishment, it was because the stage was directly plugged into life. What the spectator was seeing was his own rooms or the inside of his own head. It is important to remember how different this conception of art was from that of the neoclassicists, or even the romantics, who presumably viewed plays as achieving, or not achieving, a perfection of traditional form, a just representation of eternal nature, or as a freedom to mix forms on the theory that what was good enough for eternal nature was good enough for art. From the standpoint of the new militancy, whether expressionist or naturalist, classicism was summed up by Ernst Toller as "the expression of self-contained superior calm,"[6] and romanticism by Zola as "the restless regret of the old world."[7]

It would be absurd to conflate naturalism and expressionism as styles, or to maintain that expressionism, as a style, did not have an influence on later naturalism, as a "passion for truth." The other side of this

6. Ernst Toller, "Hoppla, Such is Life," in *Playwrights on Playwriting,* p. 226.

7. Zola, "Naturalism and the Stage," p. 117. Of course, we must bear in mind that this "organistic" idea could also be extended in the reverse direction. That is, what we are here calling naturalism cannot be cleanly separated from the "structure of feeling" of romanticism. For example, romanticism's strong theme of the imprisonment of the noble hero (e.g., Kleist's Prince of Homburg) gets carried over into naturalism in the imprisonment of the bourgeois protagonist (Hedda Gabler, the Rosmers, Ivanov) in the sociological trap of his or her living room. The romantic hero's discovery, usually while in prison, of his true self and his freedom of soul more or less disappears in naturalism and is replaced by the escape from society through the side door of suicide. (See my review of Victor Brombert's *The Romantic Prison:* "The Piranesi Effect: Alone and Well in Prison," *Hudson Review* 32 [Winter 1979–80]: 615–20). All of this, together with the passion for Truth that underlies both romanticism and naturalism, would have been a theme worth discussing here if I were writing a history of scenic illusion; but I am simply trying to illustrate the range of scenic illusion through three strong styles that may still be seen in the theater today.

argument is that expressionism (including its sister "isms"), whatever its origins in naturalistic truth seeking, represented an almost atomic release of stylistic energy. One is always impressed by the sanity of E. H. Gombrich in these duck / rabbit matters of style and content. Particularly, I think of his image of the artist as a man with a paint box and a method who goes out into nature not to paint what he sees but to see what he knows how to paint. Beyond this image of the individual talent wearing the spectacles of his own tradition, however, there is the matter of the tradition's own evolution which, though composed of a succession of individual talents, resembles a biological lifecycle. If a tradition, like an organism, is to remain vital, it follows that it must feed on something. But styles, Gombrich says, are like languages: they are inevitably limited in the number and kinds of questions they allow the artist to ask.[8] They are also, as we have said, like scientific paradigms in Thomas Kuhn's theory of scientific revolutions. And it is quite possible to see naturalism, as a rigidly mimetic style, entering a stage of crisis at about the turn of the century. There are two aspects to this crisis. The first we have discussed sufficiently: the idea that naturalism, as a style, could no longer answer the questions raised by its own discoveries (how, for example, to display what is inside the human head). The second has to do with the artistic, as opposed to the scientific problem, and it might simply be called a crisis of self-perfection. Ostensibly, the naturalist's art is marked by the disappearance of style; and though we

8. E. H. Gombrich, *Art and Illusion: A Study in the Psychology of Pictorial Representation* (New York: Pantheon Books, 1965), p. 90.

can speak, on other levels, of the style of an Ibsen or a Chekhov, naturalism was a style in which the artist disappeared, or pretended he has never been there at all. As a result, we tend to think of naturalism not as a kind of beauty but as a form of journalism which, like the newspaper, has an endless fund of new subjects and, being a thing invisible itself, is precisely as interesting as its subject's social relevance. But if we regard the theater as an institution of pleasure—that is, as something for the eye and the ear to enjoy as a species of beauty— we can see wherein naturalism was exposed to the same vicissitudes of fashion as lesser and more ostentatious movements. I say there was a crisis of self-perfection not because the world was tiring of Ibsen and Chekhov, or because there was no social work left for naturalism to do, but because there was nothing *new* it could do, as a mature style, without repeating itself to death. And it seems to be a characteristic of art movements that they must have something new to do, and as they become essentially perfect in form they sense the end of inventiveness and begin generating their own opponents or, if you wish, their own heirs.

It is usually, and in another sense quite validly, said that their opponents generate themselves on their own from the outside, like the poor rising against an aristocracy, thus giving rise to new movements. But we should not allow the noisy wars between the naturalists and the expressionists to obscure the fact that above, or beneath, all "isms" is the internal continuity of the art itself. This is implicit in Picasso's remark: "We are all Modern-Style artists. . . . Because even if you are against a movement, you're still part of it. The pro and the con are, after all, two aspects of the same move-

ment."[9] Perhaps we may describe the historical movement of an art form as a stream that flows and changes
direction at the speed of its stylistic momentum. By
this I refer to the art's ability to explore the possibilities
of its own image system—and art abhors an unused
possibility as nature abhors a vacuum—to sense the
approach of the system's collapse, to reconstitute itself
of new materials, to transmigrate, like Antony's croc-
odile, when the elements are out of it, in order to pro-
tect itself against the great deadener of its own habit.
Lurking in the word *convention,* which is art's only language, is always the danger of the conventional, or the
degeneration of the convention into unintentional self-
parody. Perhaps this is very fanciful morphology, but I
am not concerned here with giving art movements a
transcendent consciousness; rather, I am interested in
the sense in which revolutions originate from within
the stylistic paradigm, a little as the bank clerk learns
banking from the inside and then runs off with the
funds. Expressionism was an inside job in the sense
that it was prepared from naturalism's principle that
drama arises from the conflict of individuals and insti-
tutions. Expressionism did not in the least kill off naturalism, either as a style or as a structure of feeling; nor
did it affect the popularity or durability of major naturalist writers (Chekhov had barely reached Europe); it
made it possible for naturalism to remain alive, temporarily in the back seat while it reconstructed itself from
"new fundamentals," as Kuhn might say.

The difference between art paradigms and scientific

9. Françoise Gilot and Carlton Lake, *Life with Picasso* (New
York: McGraw-Hill, 1964), pp. 75–76.

paradigms is that art rarely discards any previous achievement. We do not discard naturalism as we discard the concept of a Ptolemaic universe and replace it with the "correct" Copernican view. Naturalism doesn't become invalid; it simply leads to something else and then it quietly absorbs that something else into its own practice, as we see, in different ways, in the plays of expressionists like Kaiser, Wedekind, and Strindberg, and today in the theatrical naturalism of playwrights like David Rabe, Sam Shepard, and John Guare. To sum up: with expressionism the drama abruptly reentered the world of style; moreover, a style precisely equipped to dissolve naturalism's dense centripetal mass and return the stage to the kind of epic time/space options it had enjoyed in Shakespeare's day. If expressionism, as a content, was naturalism turned inside out, as a style it was naturalism cut into pieces somewhat along the lines of Tristan Tzara's newspaper-poems: an art of sudden juxtapositions as opposed to an art of gradual transition; and most important, a style that could juxtapose various degrees of realism and nonrealism, from the filthiest cellar of hard-core naturalism to the most flagrant symbolism.

Let us take the case of Brecht as our opening onto the final phase of scenic illusion. Brecht may be said to have been born, as a theater man, between naturalism and expressionism, two mature styles that by the twenties had learned to live with each other, and to steal from each other, even to the point of becoming indistinguishable at their edges. These two styles, purely or impurely conceived, constituted the alternative languages in which one could speak from the stage. And above all else, Brecht wanted to speak. Both alternatives and, presumably, any mixture of the alternatives, were inadequate as a style for what Brecht called the "realistic" theater, or the theater that could lay bare "society's causal network."[10] As Brecht put it, "The realistic theatre has no use for the symbolism of the expressionist and existentialist stage, which expressed general ideas, nor can it turn back to the naturalist stage with its crude mixture of the relevant and the trivial. Just to copy reality isn't enough; reality needs not only to be recognized but also to be understood" (p. 233). Brecht realized what I have here tried to describe from a neutral viewpoint, that too much furniture, or walls that were too tight, created the effect of an unchangeable world, a "fated" world, much as the principle of the tragic hero led to too much "soul-probing." Naturalism, he said, promoted an atmosphere of "*tout comprendre c'est tout pardonner*" (p. 235). Expressionism, on the other hand, exposed the world "purely as a vision, strangely distorted, a monster conjured up by perturbed souls." It led to "a special kind of solipsism" (p. 132).

We are not interested here in whether Brecht was right or wrong about these styles, though it does seem reasonable to agree with Sartre that he was confront-

10. Bertolt Brecht, *Brecht on Theatre: The Development of an Aesthetic,* ed. and trans. John Willett (New York: Hill and Wang, 1966), p. 109.

ing a theater, on either extreme, that "absolutely insist[ed] on explaining things by causes and refus[ed]
to explain them by purposes."[11] And of course the fact
that he did not like expressionism's solipsistic vision
does not mean that he could not acknowledge that it
had "vastly enriched the theatre's means of expression."[12] The question is: Wherein does Brecht differ
from the expressionistic drama? It does not seem necessary to explain how he differs from naturalism. I
have argued that expressionism was a transitional
form, belonging, in different ways, to both the naturalistic and the postrealistic phase of scenic illusion.
By this I mean that it was essentially representational;
it still depicted a reality that coincided with the kind
of experience the protagonist underwent. This does
not mean that if one were to go beserk, like O'Neill's
Emperor or Kaiser's Teller, one would have just these
kinds of visual hallucinations. It means simply that scenically expressionism was, so to speak, the radiation
from a consciousness, the halo of a "perturbed soul,"
though it must be said immediately that in some
cases—notably the Strindberg of *The Ghost Sonata*—
it is hard to say whether it was the soul of the protagonist or the soul of the author that was being radiated.
On the other hand, as a scenic illusion, expressionism
undoubtedly falls into the postrealistic phase; that is,
the look of its stage, taken on face value, is stylized,
and depending on the kind and amount of scenery, you
could probably do Brecht expressionistically without

11. Jean-Paul Sartre, *Sartre on Theater,* trans. Frank Jellinek (New
York: Pantheon Books, 1976), p. 96.
12. Brecht, *Brecht on Theatre,* p. 132.

violating his play too much. Moreover, there is something vaguely expressionistic about the photos of Brecht's productions. But it does seem possible to make a *functional* distinction between expressionistic and Brechtian scenery, and the point is made very lucidly by Roland Barthes in an essay of 1956.

For what Brechtian dramaturgy postulates is that today at least, the responsibility of a dramatic art is not so much to express reality as to signify it. Hence there must be a certain distance between signified and signifier: revolutionary art must admit a certain arbitrary nature of signs, it must acknowledge a certain "formalism," in the sense that it must treat form according to an appropriate method, which is the semiological method. . . . Brecht's formalism is a radical protest against the confusions of the bourgeois and *petit-bourgeois* false Nature: in a still-alienated society, art must be critical, it must cut off all illusions, even that of "Nature": the sign must be partially arbitrary, otherwise we fall back on an art of expression, an art of essentialist illusion.[13]

13. Roland Barthes, *Critical Essays*, trans. Richard Howard (Evanston, Ill.: Northwestern University Press, 1972), pp. 74–75. We should probably take Barthes's use of the word *arbitrary* in a more or less metaphorical sense. Obviously a truly arbitrary sign, or image, in the theater would be unintelligible. Here, as elsewhere, Barthes is thinking of the signified as the referent rather than as a conceptual element of the sign itself. For example: "The notion of *product* has thus given way gradually to the notion of *sign*: the work is the sign of something beyond itself; criticism would then consist in deciphering the *signification,* in discovering its terms, and chiefly the hidden term, the thing signified [*signifié*]. . . . Who can ascertain the signifier . . . , without *first* positing the signified, *before* the signifier?" (*On Racine,* trans. Richard Howard [New York: Performing Arts Journal Publications, 1983], pp. 163–64.) In general, it seems to me that for Barthes the term *sign* implies a rejection: to say

The key word here is the one Barthes borrows from Saussurean linguistics: *arbitrary*. That is, the stylized elements on Brecht's stage (the placards, the pasteboard flats, the open lighting, the documentary materials, the provisional quality of everything) should be seen neither as the illusion of a milieu nor as an outbreak of character pathology. The setting does not grow out of the play as a fictional world, but out of an idea of which the play is simply exemplary. The scenery is intended, as Barthes says, "to infiltrate a question" into the security of stage illusion and, by extension, into the passive security of the audience. Hence, arbitrary—certainly not in the sense of capricious but in the sense of a *seeming* capriciousness that is deliberately imposed: a *certain* arbitrariness. Thus the illusion—and there can be no doubt that an illusion remains in Brecht—is continually stumbling into its own constituent parts. To put it another way, a "false Nature," the familiar Nature of a thousand bourgeois dramas, is given its semblance in the form of an honest fakery (there mustn't be any faking in the faking, Brecht says). And it is in this interval, or distance, that the Brechtian protest occurs, insofar as scenery abets the protest in the play itself.

I have a problem with this theory—that is, the theory of *Verfremdungseffekt*: it seems to take no account of the fact that distance tends to close rapidly. For exam-

that something is a sign is to look past it. Hence, for all his dependence on the word, it is an incomplete concept for his "semiological" project and, as he says in *Camera Lucida,* he borrows "something from phenomenology's project and something from its language" (p. 20). Or, again: "I am too much the phenomenologist to like anything but appearance to my own measure" (p. 33).

ple, the eye quickly becomes accustomed to light or to darkness; or, when I read the speech balloons in the comic strip, I am reading speech spoken by people in a world and not by line drawings on a page. I hear the speech; I transfer my perception to that key of signification in roughly the way that I hear the subtitles of silent films. Again, as Merleau-Ponty says, "The senses translate each other without any need of an interpreter." Similarly, in productions of Brecht it is not the stage illusion that is undercut, or even the illusion that the stage represents a certain kind of "Nature"; what is undercut is simply the conventional system of current theater. Even in Brecht, everything seeks its own illusory level: this hasty, vaguely oriental construction— "built to last precisely two hours"—becomes Shen-Te's hut; this map projection becomes Galileo's study, and then the antechamber in the Medicean palace. Even the schizophrenic actors, slightly outside their roles, playing that they are playing the roles, fade into the Brechtian illusion of theatrical protest. I see and hear a kind of reality, and the fact that I could not find its likeness the world over does not diminish the suspension of my disbelief. I still oscillate between the familiar gradients of theatrical appeal: I am moved, caught up, I feel, I think, I am bored, and I can still say to myself: "That actor is doing a good job. He has the Brecht style down pat." In other words, theater is theater.

I am not questioning Brecht's genius either as a theoretician or as a dramatist; nor do I question the suitability of his theory and practice of *Verfremdungseffekt* to his dramatic purpose in the thirties and forties. In fact, it is not Brecht I am questioning at all; rather, it is the widespread belief that there is something inherent, or fundamental, in estrangement that activates the reason as against the feelings. Brecht was no more of an aesthetician than his compatriot in protest, George Bernard Shaw. Like Shaw he wrote theory out of a deep bias and produced a perfectly coherent formula for his own uses and, most important, for his own moment in theater history. Brecht's problem was to overcome a whole century of determinism and its incalculable influence on art. The fact is that under certain conditions estrangement can activate the reason, the desire to change society, and under others it can activate the deepest resources of pity: for example, Camille's wife, in *Danton's Death,* going mad with grief for her husband against a chorus of women—a scene, so to speak, straight out of Brecht—praising the guillotine, or Mother Courage hearing the shot that kills her son and saying, "I believe—I've haggled too long." Even Schiller explained the function of the Greek chorus in Brechtian terms:

For the mind of the spectator ought to maintain its freedom through the most impassioned scenes; it should not be the mere prey of impressions, but calmly and severely detach itself from the emotions which it suffers. The commonplace objection made to the Chorus, that it disturbs the illusion, and blunts the edge of the feelings, is what constitutes its highest recommendation. . . . It is by holding asunder the different parts, and stepping between the passions with its composing views, that the Chorus restores us to our freedom, which would else be lost in the tempest.[14]

14. Friedrich Schiller, *Works,* trans. Sir Theodore Martin, Anna Swanwick, A. Lodge, and Samuel Taylor Coleridge (New York: National Library Company, 1902), 4: 231–32.

Of course this has nothing whatever to do with what one does, or thinks about, after the play is over. It is strictly the subtle *control* of the emotions for maximum aesthetic effect, like seasoning in an exquisite dish, that interests the Weimar classicist. In one way or another, the history of theater can be viewed as a history of flirtation with the psychical distance between stage and audience. Styles are reborn in new conventional disguise and certain styles serve certain purposes better than others. Sartre makes an acute point when he says that the theater of alienation is fine "if you are dealing with a society in decline" and are the spokesman for "the disinherited classes," which was substantially the case with all expressionists. But what sort of style would Brecht have developed if he had spent his artistic life inside the German Democratic Republic, sharing the general views of socialist society, but wanting to point out certain minor faults in the system?[15] The likelihood, Sartre suggests, is that he would have fallen on some variety of dramatic theater, or the theater in which "you can try to understand" why such and such a fault arises. But "in epic theater, as it is presented to us at the present time"—Sartre is writing in 1960—"you explain what you do not understand" (p. 120).

Let us turn to a case that will offer still another perspective on the theater of estrangement. Suppose that you *do* believe in an unchanging Nature, that there is a natural character of human society that survives historical process. This happens to be Thornton Wilder's position. There has rarely been a more uncritical, a more "understanding" theater. Here, if anything, we have a

15. Sartre, *Sartre on Theater*, pp. 119–20.

theater that celebrates the "false Nature" of the bourgeois; here is an art of "essentialist illusion." Yet it is a theater created out of a certain arbitrary nature of signs. A plank can become a drugstore counter, a ladder the second floor of a house, a milkman's horse can be made out of the milkman's gesture. And the characters accept these substitutions as the real thing as easily as they step out of the play to address the audience directly.

But there is, obviously, an integral relation between Wilder's scenery and his bourgeois idea of Americans living honestly and complacently in nature. What he is saying, in effect, is a variation of Brecht's principle as applied to an almost opposite purpose: if furniture, streets, and houses are "as fugitive, alas, as the years," then let us emphasize the fugitive status of these things in life; let us come right out and say that they don't matter; let us *see* that they don't matter; or, on still another level, let us see that we can see them without having them. In short, Wilder's example suggests that the "arbitrary" mode of representation does not, in itself, assure the basis of a "critical" theater. It may, indeed, have been the best kind of theater for Brecht's project, but that is a little like saying that iambic pentameter was the best kind of language for Shakespeare's. Brecht's theater, like Shakespeare's, is what he left us and one can draw no conclusions about its form being the best or the correct one for his and similar projects. Had Brecht had a temperament as unpolitical as, say, Chekhov's, he might have used the same means to create a version of estranged theater to suit quite a different sort of revolution. To come back to Wilder—whose theater was, in its way, as revolutionary as Brecht's— the theater of estrangement is simply another way (and obviously a fundamental one) of expanding the horizon of the image. It is Wilder's images that delight us, not his philosophy or the content of his plays. Some years ago we had a cinema version of *Our Town* that brought all these fugitive things to vivid life. Everything that *wasn't* on Wilder's stage—or was there only arbitrarily, at the stage manager's whim—was now, so to speak, itself: a real Our Town with trees and streets and steeples. And everything that had been fascinating about the play vanished and it became boring. What was missing, of course, was the *absence* against which all of the words and gestures in the play forge their particular validity. Throwing a real baseball into the air and shelling real peas simply trivializes these actions, in Brecht's sense, rather than casting them into relief as the permanent stuff life is made of. If there is any play that demands its meagerness, its capacity to make do with little or no means, it is this one. Wilder's is a perfect instance of a self-conscious theatricality that makes us forget we are in a theater almost as soon as it reminds us that we are. And it is out of this tension, this infinite convertibility of signs, this charm in the act of evocation, that the theater was once again able to recapture one of its ancient privileges. Shakespeare could say, "Think, when we talk of horses, that you see them," and presto! we see a certain kind of horse. Wilder could say, "This empty air is a horse because my milkman talks to it." It is the same principle of delight.

*

I suggest that if we stretch Barthes's perception about Brecht to its implicit conclusion we establish, all at once, the foundation on which the modern experimental theater is based. If we were looking for the paradigm of postnaturalist theater, in terms of its scenic appeal, what it did differently, in countless ways, to our perception of theater, we might locate it in Barthes's statement: "Revolutionary art must admit a certain arbitrary nature of signs." Of course, a semiotic approach to this revolution would hardly be very useful if it simply hangs the word *sign* on things we formerly called images. My interest here is in trying to see how the various kinds of scenic illusion may have surprised us and satisfied us in their time, and also something of how distinctions in art movements might be arrived at on the grounds of continuity rather than isolation. The semiotic approach is useful to this end because it focuses the process of theatermaking and theatergoing along the axis of cultural preparation, or what we might call the state of our perception. To broaden the point, we might put Barthes's statement beside its counterpart from Kuhn's book on scientific revolutions: "Therefore, at times of revolution, when the normal-scientific tradition changes, the scientist's perception of his environment must be re-educated—in some familiar situations he must learn to see a new gestalt" (p. 112). Bearing in mind what we have said about the inherent difference between these two kinds of revolutions, we might locate the common denominator in the problem of what vision does to vocabulary and what vocabulary does to vision. If you want to investigate a new aspect of human experience you can't use the old vocabulary of signs because, as far as expressiveness goes, the old vocabulary *is* the old experience. Obviously one can go on using the old vocabulary ironically, as Ionesco and Handke do, but the idea in such cases is to empty it in the act of using it: to show how logic and clichés accumulate to the point of chaos, or how (in *Kaspar*) the birth of the sentence is the birth of entrapment. In both of these rather specialized cases the sign system becomes almost completely arbitrary in the same sense in which the Frankenstein monster, in the old film, throws the little flower girl into the stream when he runs out of flowers. So we are not only talking about changes in words but changes in contexts as well.

What is a revolutionary artist? Every artist to some extent sees things differently and therefore does something to the art paradigm in which he works, if only to help to wear it out and prepare the ground for bolder developments. A completely nonrevolutionary art would be one that reproduced social norms in a completely normative style (one of the risks of Soviet realism). "You are normal," as Handke's Prompter puts it, "once your story is no longer distinguishable from any other story."[16] But a revolutionary artist is one who sees a *distance* between experience and the sign language of his art: "There is something art can't talk about now." We might oppose this realization to the "normal" artist's "There are still things this art can talk about" (as when the social realist, having exhausted the theme of corruption in business, daringly moves on to corruption in the palace of justice or in the church, biting off increasingly bigger chunks of forbidden reality as the theme of corruption becomes more familiar).

16. Handke, *Kaspar and Other Plays*, p. 80.

It is impossible to encompass anything as diverse as the twentieth-century revolution in experimental theater under a single principle; my case rests, however, not on the exclusivity of the principle but on its value as a perspective on a profound shift in *the function* of theater art. This shift can best be defined in terms of the liberation of the sign: a new attitude, on the part of dramatists and directors, toward the nature and use of the materials that constitute the molecular structure of theater. Expressionism was an unwitting overture to experimentalism: what the expressionist breakthrough produced, as an almost ironic by-product of its displays of social victimization and soul salvation, was the discovery that theater was not necessarily tethered to the real world. Theater was not a lively extension of the art of the novel. It had technical and affective sympathies with music, painting, and sculpture, the arts that explain themselves, as Donald Tovey says, "on the evidence of the art alone."[17] In other words, when stage imagery was freed of its servitude in mimetic signification, the one-to-one relationship between the sign and its significations, the theaters of Brecht, Meyerhold, Artaud, Wilder, the Absurdists, and Grotowski, among countless others, became possible. The distorted world of the perturbed protagonist gave way to a world distorted by the artist's personal project: an artistically mediated view of the world, but one, strangely enough, that did not set out to *express* the world or (in many cases) even to signify it, but to stand, in some degree, in its place. Here was a theater, one might say, that was about the reality of art as much as about the reality out-

17. Donald Francis Tovey, *Beethoven* (London: Oxford University Press, 1965), p.4.

side. And though theater is still in the throes of this revolution, its potential for extremity was elaborated almost immediately (1920) by the Polish dramatist-painter Stanislaw Witkiewicz:

The idea is to make it possible *to deform either life or the world of fantasy with complete freedom so as to create a whole whose meaning would be defined only by its purely scenic internal construction, and not by the demands of consistent psychology and action according to assumptions from real life. Such assumptions can only be applied as criteria to plays which are heightened reproductions of life.* Our contention is not that a play should necessarily be nonsensical, but only that from now on the drama should no longer be tied down to pre-existing patterns based solely on life's meaning or on fantastic assumptions.[18]

Witkiewicz's theory of "pure form" is not one that caught on, but in substance it is as radical a document as Artaud's *Theatre and Its Double*. In one respect it is even more radical in that it does not draw energy from any precedent form of theater (i.e., Artaud's Balinese theater) but only from those arts, music and nonrealistic painting, where pure form expressed itself as a natural function of color, line, and sound. I cite it here because it is one of the ultimate statements of modern liberation. Here we see theater, at least theoretically, rejecting the one assumption it had never disputed: the idea that it should be *about* something. In this theater—though Witkiewicz's own work, like Artaud's, never quite caught up with his theory—what occurred be-

18. Stanislaw Ignacy Witkiewicz, *The Madman and the Nun and Other Plays,* trans. Daniel C. Gerould and C. S. Durer (Seattle: University of Washington Press, 1968), pp. 292–93.

tween spectator and stage was a closed circuit of metaphysical feeling induced (Witkiewicz uses the word *injected*) by the interplay of visual and aural images. Thus the whole realm of cognition, or at least of signification of a knowable world, is bypassed. If anything, we might say that this was to be a theater about the nervous system.

It is not a very promising basis for so human an art as theater. But it bespeaks an obsession that was to infect modern theater so widely, in less extreme forms, that we may safely describe it as a key symptom of the next great revolution after naturalism. To some extent this revolution can be seen as a shift in the ground on which empathy is aroused. Empathy has always been thought of, at least in theater literature, as a sort of emotional hurling of oneself into a mirror, or what Wilhelm Worringer calls "objectified self-enjoyment"[19] (and Brecht calls "portable anguish"). At the very beginning of modern bourgeois drama, Beaumarchais defined empathy, or what he called "interest," as the "involuntary feeling through which we adapt ourselves to an event, the feeling which puts us in the place of someone who suffers, in the midst of his situation."[20] Even Brecht

19. Wilhelm Worringer, *Abstraction and Empathy: A Contribution to the Psychology of Style,* trans. Michael Bullock (New York: International Universities Press, 1953), p. 5. The context of the term is: "To enjoy aesthetically means to enjoy myself in a sensuous object diverse from myself, to empathize myself into it." This, of course, is a restatement of Theodor Lipps's theory of empathy in *Aesthetik* (Hamburg and Leipzig: L. Voss, 1903).

20. Pierre Augustin Caron de Beaumarchais, "Essai sur Le Genre Dramatique Sérieux," in *Oeuvres complètes de Beaumarchais,* Nouvelle édition (Paris: Laplace, Sanchez etc. Cⁱᵉ, Libraires Éditeurs, 1876), p. 3. My translation.

could not get empathy entirely out of his theory, and certainly not out of his art. But empathy thus defined (and aroused) is a condition deriving from the representational function of art: "This man's situation could be mine," or "I weep when he weeps," and by Brecht's extension, "I stop weeping when the play is over"— that is, I have my catharsis and go home, purged. Altogether, we could call this the empathy of situation, or, in view of our interest here, the empathy of signification, since its basis lies in a mirrorlike reflection of sign and signified. One can see why the bourgeois naturalist devoted himself to the production of this kind of empathy and why Brecht sensed that the very marrow of his enemy was to be found in its soothing agitations.

But can art ever deliver itself from empathy? Isn't empathy the force that keeps us in our theater seats? In short, a kind of sensory self-projection, or willingness to vibrate in tune with the work, with whatever the work may be up to. On this level, empathy disappears only when beauty disappears, when the play makes a mistake, when the acting is bad, or when an accident occurs on stage, and we come back, prematurely, to ourselves. Could we not say that Brecht was actually exorcising one kind of empathy in order to admit another? Not empathy in any sense of the "bourgeois" definition but empathy cleansed of class flattery: exactly the kind of empathy we find in the work of one of the painters who apparently inspired him the most, Brueghel the Elder. Here we have a criticism of the world *without comment,* by such irony as can depict the diminutive figure of Christ en route to Golgotha— which speaks for itself—almost lost in a sea of festivity. It is the lostness of the sacrifice that draws us into the painting emotionally; it is the festivity that draws us back, but not *out of* the work, and makes us think: passion framed by an idea, both framed in art. In technique, it is the same brand of irony that Swift used to expose British inhumanity, and its premise is the report of a human outrage in an absolutely level (if not genial) voice. Brecht himself spoke of this as a fusion of the contradiction between acting (demonstration) and experience (empathy).[21] To return to the death of Swiss Cheese: here is one of Brecht's most Brueghelesque moments, and what makes it so wrenching is that it contains no emotional reference to its own emotion. But the fact that it doesn't serve up our emotions for us does not mean that it isn't producing them. It was not a pitiless man who conceived this scene—and especially that masterfully underslung line, "I believe . . . I've haggled too long"—but a poet who knew that human loss would speak for itself in a context of stupidity and greed.[22] It is not a question here simply of being sympathetic to Mother Courage, or of putting ourselves in her situation, but of being unable to reconcile the most

21. Brecht, *Brecht on Theatre*, p. 277.

22. One might say of Brecht's tone what Rolf Breuer says of the "cold" poetry of Gottfried Benn: "Is it not rather that there prevails in his poems an aversion to hawking that cheapest of all goods, emotion (well-meaning as it may be)? One must surely understand the apparent coldness as a façade; one must read the poems as being filled with sympathy—though sympathy under complete control. The poet covers his face with the mask of neutrality only because he does not want his own or his readers' emotions to distract from his subject. Here, then, irony serves the purpose of laying bare the subject matter, and the laying bare of the subject shows its ironical structure" ("Irony, Literature, and Schizophrenia," *New Literary History* 12 [Autumn 1980]: 113).

primal of losses with a behavior that could both bring it about and suffer for it. We are caught in a typical Brecht contradiction. If Courage were less of a contradiction herself, we would have a trivial situation: if she were, on one hand, more the businesswoman, she would be an uninteresting abomination; if she were, on the other hand, more the loving mother, we would feel only a bathos of the sort that Dumas *fils* often arranged. But as Brecht draws her, we are suspended in an Aristotelian paradox: she elicits both pity, the impulse to approach or to understand, and fear, the impulse to retreat (though in Brecht's critical theater we must substitute another word for tragic fear, perhaps outrage, in the sense that we know "this should not be!"). But it is through this balance of conflicting feelings, of empathy and objectivity, that Brecht avoids the excesses of sentimentality and moral didacticism and creates a form of classical theater. This is not what Brecht had in mind, but it is what will make his plays producible long after *Verfremdungseffekt* is a dead word.

What character does empathy assume when the artist loses interest in man as a primarily social being? I want to pursue this question briefly through two exemplary theaters that stand, in form and mission, almost opposite the theater of Brecht. I speak of Artaud and Grotowski, who are the most obvious choices, perhaps, but also the best if we are to illustrate the extremes of empathy in the theater of the estranged sign. There is no need for still another descriptive analysis of either of these theaters, since they are so well-known and influential. Here we are interested only in a particular *kind* of phenomenological relation between means and ends, and on this level we can treat Artaud and Grotowski as almost interchangeable.

Jacques Derrida has written a superb semiological analysis of Artaud's theater, but here I want to turn to his commentary on Rousseau in *Of Grammatology* where the theater enters a discussion of "presence" and "the profound evil of re-presentation." In theater, as in writing, Derrida says (speaking, in part, for Rousseau), "the visible signifier has always already begun to separate itself from speech and to supplant it."[23] Unlike the orator,

the actor is born out of the rift between the representer and the represented. Like the alphabetic signifier, like the letter, the actor himself is not inspired or animated by any particular language. He signifies nothing. He hardly lives, he lends his voice. It is a mouthpiece. Of course the difference between the orator or preacher and the actor presupposes that the former does his duty, says what he has to say. If they do not assume ethical responsibility for their word, they become actors, hardly even actors, for the latter make a duty of saying what they do not think (p. 305).

Here, of course, we reach a much more basic level of arbitrariness than Barthes had in mind: theater itself, being doomed to this zone of artificiality and pretense, is the very essence of self-annihilation and, for Rousseau, the playful extension of everything that is artificial in

23. Jacques Derrida, "From /Of the Supplement to the Source: The Theory of Writing," in *Of Grammatology*, trans. Gayatri C. Spivak (Baltimore: Johns Hopkins Press, 1980), p. 304.

society. In no public institution is the corruption of alienation more deeply dramatized. First, the theater is
doubly representational in the sense that its text represents a fiction *about* society and its medium is a mouthpiece for the text; second, *presence,* in the sense of something speaking *for* and *as* itself, is abolished. Theater is a
re-presentation, a re-presence (if that), perfected in the
rehearsal process and locked into the fraud of self-repeti-
tion. For Rousseau, the alternative to the theater, to representation, was the outdoor public festival, where
there was no play, no show, no masks, no substitution of
one thing for another, only a space where "each sees and
loves himself in the others," where one might find "that
lost unity of glance and speech," where one might
"again *listen to himself*" (p. 304).

But, as Derrida says, "the relationship of natural to
artificial or arbitrary is itself subject to the law of 'extremes' which 'touch one another'" (p. 302). In other
words, to carry the argument beyond Rousseau to our
immediate subject, it is possible that the very falsity of
the theater might serve as the scene for a "presence" if
theater could give up its spectacle of fakery and likeness,
of being the carrier of a message (wherein Brecht found
its greatest strength), and somehow *be itself*—or, more
accurately, find the subject of its re-presentation in the
living substance of its own body. In passing, Derrida
notes that some of Rousseau's propositions for the public
festival might be realized in Artaud's theater of cruelty.
One could turn almost anywhere in Artaud and find
echoes of the festival principle. I take one passage in particular, not as the best description of the theater of cruelty, but as an expression of this homing instinct as it
bears on scenic illusion:

It has not been definitively proved that the language of words is the best possible language. And it seems that on the stage, which is above all a space to fill and a place where something happens, the language of words may have to give way before a language of *signs* whose objective aspect is the one that has the most immediate impact upon us.

Considered in this light, the objective work of the *mise en scène* assumes a kind of intellectual dignity from the effacement of words behind gestures and from the fact that the esthetic, plastic part of theatre drops its role of decorative intermediary in order to become, in the proper sense of the word, a directly communicative *language*.[24]

The basis of this theater is that the stage becomes "the most active and efficient *site of passage*" of "ideas into things" (p. 109). Gesture, sound, objects, everything, especially words, will have "approximately the importance they have in dreams" (p. 94), the creative medium par excellence, in which *anything* may serve as an image for the preoccupation of the dream artist. The thing emphasized throughout Artaud's theory is its war against the tyranny of reference, or at least reference to the social world from which man, as dreamer, is automatically excluded. Theater must be a "reconquest of the signs of what exists" (p. 63). Its object is to strip signs, to empty them of received content and to reconstitute them as a beginning or, in Rousseau's word, as a birth. It is what we might loosely call a *phenomenological theater* (as opposed to semiological) in that it seeks to retrieve a naive perception of the thing—its "objective aspect"—before it was defined out of sight by language. As Grotowski put it, writing about Artaud,

24. Artaud, *The Theater and Its Double*, p. 107.

"The theatre is an act carried out *here and now* in the actors' organisms, in front of other men. . . . Theatrical reality is instantaneous, not an illustration of life but something linked to life *only by analogy*."[25]

Grotowski's theory evolves from the idea that what most distinguishes theater from film and television is "the closeness of the living organism" (p. 41). Hence the less distance between actor and audience the better; the content of this theater will be myths of the blood (p. 42) rather than fictions bearing on social life and behavior. One might say that representation, in Grotowski's theater, is the presentation of the being (body and soul) of the audience in the person of the actor who stands in roughly the relation of Christ to man in the Passion. In this sacrificial closeness, the audience—deliberately kept small—watches its delegate, not its likeness, one who is there not for the spectator but simply *instead of* him (p. 131).

As a consequence of this mission of transcendence of "the half measures of daily life" (p. 131), the *mise en scène* now has the function of releasing the intense creative force of the actor. There is an almost neoclassic stringency in Grotowski's insistence on poverty of means in his theater. Usually, rules (for example, the three unities) are means of provoking virtuosity (either of dramatist or performer) on the theory that a triumph must be a triumph *over* something. The dead end of naturalism is that it was not possible to have an art of the actor, as a presence, as long as the actor's virtuosity consisted in disappearing, like a chameleon, into the environ-

25. Jerzy Grotowski, *Towards a Poor Theatre* (New York: Simon and Schuster, 1969), p. 118.

ment. In historical perspective, we may say that Grotowski's theater, more so than Artaud's, was a means of
making the actor once again the pivot of the spectacle.
And whereas Artaud's tendency was to see scenery as
one means, among many, of "ensnaring the organs" of
the audience, Grotowski thought of scenery (or what
scenery he permitted) as a tool standing in a host relation to the parasite actor. For example, in *Akropolis:*

There are no "sets" in the usual sense of the word. They have
been reduced to the objects which are indispensable to the
dramatic action. Each object must contribute not to the
meaning but to the dynamics of the play; its value resides in
its various uses. The stovepipes and the metallic junk are
used as settings and as a concrete, three-dimensional metaphor which contributes to the creation of the vision. But the
metaphor originates in the function of the stovepipes; it
stems from the activity which it later supersedes as the function progresses. When the actors leave the theatre, they leave
behind the pipes which have supplied a concrete motivation
for the play. . . . We are dealing with a theatre caught in its
embryonic stage, in the middle of the creative process when
the awakened instinct chooses spontaneously the tools of its
magic transformation. A living man, the actor, is the creative force behind it all (pp. 75–76).

There are obviously problems with any theater demanding such visceral spontaneity. Probably the big-
gest is the old menace of repetition: How could one do
Artaud *again,* night after night, assuming one could do
him at all? Is it possible that the dream text of the theory itself, a theater for the most part in Artaud's head,
was its own best and unsurpassable performance? And

surely there are evenings when Ryzard Cieslak, a "living man" after all, does not *feel* like giving birth to himself; surely there are times when he slips into doing this *for* the audience rather than *instead* of the audience. The important point, for our history, is the vision itself, the penetration (a key Grotowski word) of still another layer of unarticulated sensation beneath the shell of familiar truth. ("The interior," as Heidegger says of the broken piece of chalk, "is really only an exterior lying farther back."[26]) Above all, such a project, in any of its countless variations, involved a radical shift in the empathetic basis of theater. Let us briefly return to naturalism to see what this shift amounts to. The pleasure of naturalism may be likened to the pleasure of miniature which allows us to see a replica of the familiar world contained, as we can never see it while we are in it (there would be little point in a miniature of something we did not recognize). The making small of miniature is equivalent to naturalism's frontal dollhouse view. In naturalism, as in miniature, we play the voyeur: we enter the world through the keyhole of the eye; in one sense we hide in it, in another we oversee it, marveling at the capacity of art to be so meticulous an imitator of things. The paradox of miniature and naturalism is that they consolidate both our intimacy with the world and our distance from it. We become world-conscious, as Bachelard says, "at slight risk."[27]

The pleasure of this new theater, as articulated by Artaud and Grotowski, is the pleasure of magic, trance,

26. Martin Heidegger, *What Is a Thing?*, trans. W. B. Barton and Vera Deutsch (South Bend, Ind.: Gateway Editions, 1967), p. 21.

27. Bachelard, *The Poetics of Space,* p. 161.

and participation. Distance, even the mildest suspension in voyeurism, is incompatible with it; for above all this theater aims at reaching us below the threshold of critical thought, and this is the principal respect in which it stands opposite Brecht's theater. ("Alienation," Derrida says in his essay on Artaud, "only consecrates, with didactic insistence and systematic heaviness, the nonparticipation of spectators (and even of directors and actors) in the creative act, in the irruptive force fissuring the space of the stage."[28]) What is solicited here, to update Coleridge, is the willing suspension of our self-isolation. The magic that Artaud and Grotowski talk about is that of transformation or alchemy; it is not only that the eye can be tricked into seeing almost any object as something else, but that an object that does not represent something *in advance* becomes a blank check, an open presence; it becomes the source of something *not yet here,* a thing without a history, or rather a thing whose history is about to be revised. This is the grim magic behind the common bathtub that serves as a processing vat for human corpses one minute and an altar the next, or a simpleton gradually transformed into the Christ. In purely visual terms, this is the participatory ground of Grotowski's theater, and one can already see its affinities with Shakespeare's theater of the verbal metaphor. What is unrealistic about Shakespeare's theater, finally, is that it is constantly dealing in principles, in transformations, rather than in replicas: nothing comes to rest in itself; everything calls forth *other* manifestations of its shape, size, quality, or mood. Who could escape being drawn into this world as one that is constantly being made and

28. Derrida, "The Theater of Cruelty," p. 244.

remade, endlessly illustrating the laws of combinability, endlessly putting us in the interstice of a metaphor?

In an essay on the nature of metaphor, Ted Cohen suggests that metaphor, among its various uses, serves in the achievement of intimacy: "The maker and the appreciator of a metaphor are drawn closer to one another." The maker issues a "concealed invitation" (the metaphor); the hearer (or onlooker) accepts and extends the effort of a special attentiveness, and "this transaction constitutes the acknowledgment of a community."[29] This had never occurred to me, but Cohen's is one of those modest suggestions that immediately verifies, or identifies, a host of old feelings. Of course Cohen isn't arguing that metaphor can't reverse its emotional field and become ironic and nasty. But with the right intentions, it can work like a secret password or handshake known only to insiders. And *this* metaphor leads me directly to the set of metaphors that crops up over and again in Artaud, Grotowski, Peter Brook, the Becks, Richard Schechner, et al.: I refer to such terms, applied to the theater, as ritual, ceremony, rite, myth, liturgy, cult, initiation, etc. In other words, the pleasure of this intimacy consists in the invitation to the audience to share a world of spirit and feeling that one enters only by first sharing—to speak metaphorically—in the death of the old language (symbolized by the "death" of the bathtub-vat and the simpleton) and the creation of a new one (symbolized by the "birth" of the bathtub-altar and the Christ figure). I don't mean that the experience is always a religious one, only that

29. Ted Cohen, "Metaphor and the Cultivation of Intimacy," *Critical Inquiry* 5 (Autumn 1978): 8.

religious imagery best expresses the mission of this theater: to unite the body of the actor and the soul of the audience in an act of discovery. In this sense the intimate theater is part of the "eternal web of Penelope" of the modern avant-garde, to invoke Renato Poggioli's image[30]: it must constantly begin again, from scratch, constantly unweave its own history in an effort to remain a *presence,* rather than a supplement to itself.

30. Renato Poggioli, *The Theory of the Avant-Garde,* trans. Gerald Fitzgerald (New York: Harper & Row, 1971), p. 82.

Part Two

The Actor

4

Actor / *Text*

The inevitable starting point of any discussion of the actor's presence on the stage is the fact that we see him as both character and performer. One of the reasons that it may be easier to become lost in a film than in an enacted play is that the film removes the *actual* aspect of performance and leaves us with the record of an actuality into which we can safely sink. But in the theater our sympathetic involvement with the characters is attended by a secondary, and largely subliminal, line of empathy born of the possibility that the illusion may at any moment be shattered by a mistake or an accident. For the most part this is a low-risk investment, but it is a crucial aspect of the phenomenal quality of stage performance. It is our creatural bond with the actor, who stands before us in a vulnerable place. When we applaud the actor at the end of the play we imply that he "became" his character well: we were moved not by a performance but by the illusion the performance signified. But we also applaud him for successfully passing through the pitfalls of his role. Virtuosity, in theater as in athletics, is not simply skill but skill displayed against odds which, when mastered, become beautiful passages. To round out the comparison, one might liken the film actor to the aerialist who works with a net. His performance is no less a thing of beauty than that of the stage actor, but it is relieved of all possibility of disaster except that of poor acting. But the theater offers the actor no net: the play is one long danger. The danger in *Lear* is located exactly in its beauty. What actor has ever approached "Blow winds and crack your cheeks" without knowing that he must become a sublime tempest without exhausting the reserve needed to scale the mountain of verse to follow? What actor has ever approached the "solid flesh" soliloquy—Hamlet is finally *alone* on stage!—without knowing that here, in one speech, he confronts Hamlet's awesome range and depth, the pitch pipe of the entire character to which the court-scene asides were but preface and promise? Hamlet's own advice to the players about "natural" acting, suiting the action to the word, implies a temperance in the delivery that is ultimately aimed at putting the actor, as a real stranger, at home in the unreal world of the play. One might even say that the text ceases to exist when it is naturally spoken by the actor, but exists too plentifully when the actor mouths his lines.

Let us say we are attending a performance of *Hamlet*. The actor to play Hamlet—not yet Hamlet—is seen for the first time in the second scene. We have not seen this actor's work before. He does not, therefore, look like Hamlet, like *a* Hamlet, like the ideal image we have in mind for Hamlet. He is too squat, or too tall, not right for the role. He speaks, "A little more than kin. . . ," and his voice is too high. So we have the impression of a stranger speaking Hamlet's lines; the real Hamlet instantly retreats to literature, becomes a mouthed text floating in and out as the actor finds him in certain phrases and loses him in others. The text becomes too plentiful, too familiar. But it is not as bad as that. Gradually, we become used to Hamlet in this form. It was not actually the acting that threw us out of the play or did not allow us in. It was a version of the same process of wearing-in that occurs, say, when we fall in love. That is, the purely gratuitous mixture of facial features, voice, manner, etc., gradually—in some cases, suddenly—becomes inevitable, a synthesis expressive of something ideal, irresistible. The same is true, of course, when we "fall into hate" with someone: the person simply becomes correlative with a feeling.

So Hamlet consents to settle into this mortal who, by dint of his unique skill and presence, earns the part. But it has been a contest for possession in which the actor-character teeters constantly on the verge of catastrophe—that is, of becoming one of us. Actors refer to this as *falling* out of character, a highly expressive metaphor for this sudden entry into the lower, or nonabsolute, world of the audience. Obviously, this is too severe. Actors do not feel they are in danger in the sense that a demolition expert does. The danger the actor experiences is necessary if there is to be an art of acting. It is the opponent for which the actor is thankful, like the aerialist's high wire or the mountaineer's rock face. It is what he works with, and for. It is the condition of virtuosity.

It is no wonder that we have the cliché of the egotistical actor. If we are amazed at the phenomenon of the shy actor (one of the pleasant discoveries of the TV talk show), it is only because it strikes us as a behavioral oxymoron. How is it possible to be shy when one has so deliberately sought the attention of the world? It is not necessary to defend the proposition that there are more egotistical actors than funeral directors or postmen to see the truth in the cliché. It has nothing to do with vanity, or with showing off, however much the actor may be lured to these shallows by the rewards of his profession. The egotism of the actor expresses itself categorically in the simple fact that he risks the stage. To venture into this realm of massive personalities is to ask boldly to be compared to Hamlet. In this realm, his ego could not possibly be one that puffs itself visibly, for in the theater there is nothing worse than vain acting. If anything, the actor's appearance before the world is the essence of tact and selflessness. (We will take up a possible exception to this notion later.) He succeeds to the degree that his ego is thoroughly "laundered," as the politicians say, by his project: the assumption of another ego. If the role is a constant danger, it is also a perfect shield behind which he disappears and reappears as an incarnation. Even his personal imperfections (a long nose, a thin voice) are left behind—that is, converted into the givens of a unique characterization. By contrast, what is so offensive about the muscleman (at least to those outside the circle of the art) is that he comes on his stage, as Nietzsche says of the primitive conqueror, *bare of pretext*.[1] His body, the product of an extraordinary discipline, is put to no use: it becomes nothing else, it presents nothing beyond its own grotesque possibilities. And because there is no pretext, no shield, the muscleman's display is the incarnation of vanity.

But this idea of the actor's disappearing act is not altogether satisfying. Somehow we have not really coaxed the actor's way of speaking and being before us

1. Nietzsche, *The Birth of Tragedy*, p. 220.

out of its own inwardness when we have said that he "annihilates himself" (Rousseau) in the character. Another way of approaching the ontology of the actor is to consider him as a kind of storyteller whose specialty is that he *is* the story he is telling. Presumably, the transitional voice between the true storyteller and the actor would be the rhapsode who tells his story (or rather someone else's) directly to the audience, simulating the more exciting parts of it in the manner of the First Player in *Hamlet* who gets so carried away by the plight of Hecuba. With the actor, of course, the narrative voice ("Anon he finds him striking too short at Greeks") disappears entirely and we hear only the fictitious first-personal voice ("Now I am alone," or "Now, mother, what's the matter?")—rather, we *over*hear it, since the voice is no longer speaking to us. The audience is now an implicit or unacknowledged "you," at least in the more naturalistic styles of acting. This is, of course, what bothered Rousseau so much, that the actor was the final step in the disintegration of presence and direct discourse.

I cite this familiar evolution only so that we might regain some sense of the narrator hiding in the actor, just as there is an actor hiding in the rhapsode. What distinguishes the First Player in the Pyrrhus speech from the complete actor he will become that same evening in *The Murder of Gonzago* is simply that in one case he is carried away by a fiction, and in the other he is carried away in, or as, a fiction: in one case he observes, in the other he becomes. In either case, the indispensable personal pronominal order of all discourse holds: speaker (I), spoken to (you), and spoken of (he). We can

make better sense of this idea if we put it in the form of
a chart opposing the world of the theater and the
fictional world of the play along the pronominal axis.
Since Jiri Veltrusky has already given us terms for these
two "worlds," let us refer to them as "the acting event"
and "the enacted event"[2]:

THEATER (Acting event)			PLAY (Enacted event)
Actor	=	I	= Character
Audience =		you	= Other characters or self
Character =		he (it)	= Absent character or events

The Play column speaks for itself: characters in a play
speak, as we do in life, to each other (dialogue) or to
themselves (soliloquy) about events or about people
(usually absent). The Theater column, however, requires a shift in perspective on the speech process. In
sum: the actor (I) speaks to the audience (you) about the
character (he) he is playing. By extension, the ensemble of actors in any play would constitute the plural
number of this same order of speech (we-you-they).
But how is this possible? How does the actor speak to
the audience *about* the character he is playing?

Immediately we see that the *I* of the actor is not at all
the *I* of the character he is playing, the voice that keeps
saying, "I, I, I" throughout the play. The actor's first
person is what appears before us *as* the character, the
being that has, in effect, no voice of its own but whose
very presence and way of appearing constitute the act

2. Jiri Veltrusky, "Contribution to the Semiotics of Acting," in
Sound, Sign, and Meaning (Ann Arbor: University of Michigan
Press, 1976), p. 572.

of direct speech within the indirect speech in the enacted event. It is visible in the effortless hard work that
produces on the actor's brow beads of perspiration that
do not belong to the character. But the *I* is not simply
the actor's real body. It is rather the unnatural attitude
of the body, the thousand different means and behavioral peculiarities by which the actor unavoidably remains just outside the character he is playing. He is always slightly quoting his character, though not as
Brecht's actor practices quoting—that is, not as a consciously estranged style. Even if he is quoting in the
Brechtian sense, there is a quotation beyond this quotation. No matter how he acts, there is always the ghost
of a self in his performance (not to be confused with
egotism). Even the most unsophisticated theatergoer
can detect something else in the characterization, a su-
perconsciousness that could be nothing other than the
actor's awareness of his own self-sufficiency as he
moves between the contradictory zones of the illusory
and the real, *vraisemblance* and *vrai,* seeming and being—between Hamlet and what of himself he has allowed to be displayed as Hamlet. It is not a statement
made by the body or the eyes, but an intentional edge
in the performance, signified by the aura of style and
concentration, or by the submission of the body to a
certain rigor, or absence of excess, that relieves the
most naturalistic performance of a completely convincing realism. It is something that could not be found in
any other form than that of art.

Among Kierkegaard's aesthetic writings on the theater there is a sentence that perfectly describes this hovering self of the actor as the character passes through
him—in this case, through *her,* since the model in ques-

tion is a Danish actress who, in Kierkegaard's view, had played Shakespeare's Juliet to perfection on the Copenhagen stage at the age of thirty-four. "Not only does she take the author's words correctly off his lips," Kierkegaard says, "but she gives them back to him in such a way, in the accompanying sound of her playfulness and the self-awareness of her own genius, that she seems to say in addition: . . . . Here is the original you were trying to copy."[3]

How can we imagine the actress as seeming to say this as she performs? By what audacity can she steal the playwright's line and call it her own, rather than her character's? Again, it is important to avoid any suggestion that she does this visibly or by winking, so to speak, from behind the shield of her character; or, moreover, that her aside contains the slightest insinuation of smugness or superiority (*playfulness*, we must add, has a very special meaning for Kierkegaard, far too complex to explore here). It comes simply, as Kierkegaard says, with being "in league with ideality," with being "in the right rapport with *the tension* of the stage" (p. 77, emphasis mine). It is at once a solidity and a buoyancy: it is what art would say if art had a voice.

What it seems to me that Kierkegaard truly ex-

3. Søren Kierkegaard, *Crisis in the Life of an Actress and Other Essays on Drama*, trans. Stephen Crites (London: Collins, 1967), p. 77. Actually, the text of the actress's sentence in the translation reads: "Let me see you copy that." I have substituted the paraphrase the translator suggests in his notes (p. 131)—"Here is the original you were trying to copy"—because it seems to me far richer in its implications. If Kierkegaard did not say this exactly (the Danish reads: *kan Du gjøre mig det efter*), one could certainly derive it from his portrait of the ideal actress.

presses here is the actor's creatural awareness that he is the theater's natural and only conduit. He is the original of the poet's "copy" in the sense that *he is the being who grants it an existence.* The poet may have conceived the words, but insofar as they are true they are borrowed from nature; they are what he heard as his imagination listened to the world. To this degree, all dramatic texts are hypotheses, yearnings. The poet records his vision of the world as an imitation of a possible truth. And behold, the actor appears and validates his vision, as nature validates the vision of the physicist by behaving naturally. The actor is living proof that the play is true: he takes the words from the poet's lips and gives them back, causing him to say, like Voltaire on hearing Clairon in his play, "*Did I really write that?*"[4] In other words, the poet's copy falls *into* nature in the form of a demonstration. One might say that in becoming Hamlet or Juliet the actor throws himself into the gap between the hypothetical and the real.

In this light, the ancient association of actor and prostitute is justified: the actor is someone who consents to be used; one text is the same as another. This has nothing to do with a promiscuity of taste or an indifference to the size or quality of the role, but with the fact that all roles make the same demand on the actor's person. Osric or Hamlet, it is but two dishes to one table, the same act of self-displacement and self-containment carried out, as Kierkegaard says, under "the prodigious burden" of "the weight of everyone's eyes" (p. 77). Here, perhaps, is the true source of the

4. As quoted in Denis Diderot, *The Paradox of Acting* (New York: Hill and Wang, 1967), p. 42.

sacrificial depth of playing: the actor is someone like us who consents to serve as the channel through which the poet's art can be brought out of the realm of imitation and briefly detained, for our narcissistic pleasure, in the realm of being.

We must pursue further the question of how the channel of the actor's body influences the nature and rigor of the dramatic text that passes through it. There are really two questions here, or at least two perspectives from which we can ask the question: the first pertains to the actor's influence on the composition of the dramatic text—in a word, how the dramatist composes, as we say, *for* the actor as the inevitable carrier of his text; the second pertains to what the actor's presence does *to* the text as it passes through him, transcending textuality and becoming a theatrical representation. Although we are speaking here primarily of the "literary" theater for which plays are written, one might argue that even in most forms of improvisational theater the actor is performing only what he has, in Hamlet's phrase, "set down" for himself to improvise. In other words, there is normally at least a playwright *function* in theater, or the hand of a playwright who has prepared the text (or is preparing one before our eyes) which the actor performs. From the phenomenological standpoint, the text is not a prior document; it is the animating current to which the actor submits his body and refines himself into an illusionary being. In other words, it is by virtue of the absent text that the actor becomes a real person living, as Sartre puts it, in an unreal way.[5]

In order to deal with the first problem—how the dramatist composes *for* the actor—let us define a play as an exercise for realizing the possibilities of the actor. I have taken this idea, in principle, from Francis Fergusson's essay on the histrionic sensibility in *The Idea of a Theater,* and specifically from this passage: "A technique of acting . . . merely leads to the literature of drama, just as the performer's technique of the violinist leads to the literature of the violin, where the possibilities of the instrument are explored."[6] Here I wish to develop a slightly different aspect of the relation of actor to stage literature: it is not simply the artist's technique that leads to the literature but the instrument itself, though obviously a certain technique of acting may encourage a certain kind of play (as the development of realistic acting may be said to have encouraged more realistic plays). Any approach to this idea must treat the actor synchronically, outside of the historical evolution of acting styles and dramatic forms; for there is no law of the actor, or of the dramatic text, or of their symbiotic relationship, that is not constantly amended by the fashions and enthusiasms of culture. What is a good actable text for the actor of one age may become a difficult one for the actor in another. Presumably, however, beneath the historical march of styles, techniques, and forms, the actor remains the indispensable instrument on which the music of theater is played, and like all instruments it is inherently limited in its versatility

5. Sartre, *Psychology of Imagination,* p. 250.
6. Francis Fergusson, *The Idea of a Theater* (Garden City, N. Y.: Doubleday & Co., 1949), p. 253.

by its physical construction. Consequently, if the playwright writes for the actor, he must abide by certain "rules of nature." But this statement requires some worrying past the cliché that plays are not complete works of art until they are put on stage by actors. Shakespeare, theater people are pleased to note, was an actor; he wrote for the stage and went to his peace caring little about the survival of his texts, even for future actors' use. His plays—and by extension all plays—are essentially scripts, or scores, that exist only in a literary limbo until actors, the musicians of the tribe, arrive and give them sound and sensible motion. This is an innocent enough fiction, notwithstanding the fact that there are as many things about *Hamlet* one cannot possibly appreciate in a performance as there are things in a performance that elude the most sensitive reading. But this has less to do with art than with biopsychology— that is, with the range of responses awakened by different senses and stimuli.

It would come closer to the nature of the histrionic sensibility to say that the playwright himself becomes the actor in the act of writing. Let us say, for instance, that in creating the character of Hamlet Shakespeare had Richard Burbage in mind: he gave Hamlet some of Burbage's mannerisms; he saw Hamlet moving like Burbage and heard Burbage's voice when he composed Hamlet's lines. But surely there was a point at which Shakespeare went beyond Burbage, lost sight of him altogether and began following Hamlet, like Hamlet following the Ghost, into a mist of Hamlet-possibilities in which Burbage would inevitably have to follow and shift for himself. In other words, Shakespeare found within himself the behavioral pattern for Hamlet. This has nothing to do with putting his own character into Hamlet, any more than it does with putting it into Polonius or Osric. He simply worked out Hamlet's possibilities on the instrument of his own organism, as Grotowski would say, the same act of self-extension that would later attend Burbage's preparation and enactment of the role. One might say that Burbage was the *second* actor to perform Hamlet. Moreover, bearing in mind that the playwright always has one eye on the interests and tolerances of the society for which he writes, one might say that in conceiving Hamlet Shakespeare condensed in his own person the roles of dramatist, actor, and audience. In fact, without being all three of these beings at once a playwright can scarcely be said to be writing for the theater —one factor, among many, that separates Shakespeare from, say, Seneca, Coleridge, and Gordon Bottomley.

Composing for the actor, whether for the actor within oneself or the actor in one's theater company, means simply composing for the human instrument with all its stops and ventages. Thus everything that takes place on the stage, apart from scenic and sound effects, must be impersonated. Henry James's notion that character and event are simply two different names for the same thing becomes at once the strict condition of theater's limitations and the source of its special virtuosity. Character and plot—and we must add that third "object of imitation," *thought*—meet and become virtually indistinguishable in the body of the actor.[7]

7. I am of course revising Aristotle's idea that we can neatly separate character, thought, and plot. Aristotle felt that character was exhibited only in speeches in which moral choices were made, and not in speeches in which the character was simply stating an opinion, proving a point or a general principle. In our modern concept

What the drama gains, therefore, in actuality, in the objective presence of its illusion, it loses in versatility of medium and representational capability. Hence the peculiar quality of theater as the art that has no privileged voice. By voice we mean not only that there is no *sound* of a storyteller—even one so inaudible as the "he said"s of prose fiction—but that there is no narrative means through which our own view can be expanded or reduced and focused on the macro- or microlevels of behavior and action. For example, on the macrolevel, the drama cannot fight wars very well. Battles are waged, but we see, in Hugo's phrase, only "the elbows of the action"; that is, a brief synecdochic alarum, just enough to get the plot through an event that is more properly viewed by the all-seeing eye of the epic or the film. One would hardly say, as a consequence, that the drama cannot catch the sweep of war and the collapse of nations, but that is a function of how well it is able to convert a handful of individual passions into an illusion of social movement. Nor, on the microlevel, can the drama explore the depth of the mind too scrupulously; for the drama will tolerate nothing of the psychological or philosophical that is not expressed in visible action. We often praise Shakespeare's soliloquies for their depth of thought, but we are probably confusing depth and eloquence, or at least depth of thought with depth of feel-

---

of character there can scarcely be a scene (much less an entire play) in which the characters do not exhibit character, if only because they stand or sit in a particular way. Perhaps one should draw a distinction between character (in the ethical sense) and personality (in the sense of personal traits of behavior).

ing. Even a character as philosophical as Hamlet can hardly be called a profound thinker on the evidence of his thoughts. Any one of them might serve as the epigraph for an entire philosophy of existence or ethical responsibility, but we never catch him tracking an idea that does not cast his whole being (and hence the actor's) into a visible attitude. In short, philosophy, in the theater, must unfold itself, literally, as a thinking of the body.

Let us take the simplest possible illustration of drama passing through the actor and see where it leads us in drama's peculiar textual world. Here is a passage from Ibsen in which nothing much is happening. The play is simply behaving like any play in its early stages, casually, subtly, putting out its world-lines, creating not so much its major anticipations as the energies that will trigger them in due course.

MISS TESMAN: You don't seem to have wasted your time on your wedding trip!

TESMAN: Indeed I haven't!—But do take off your hat, Aunt Juliane—let me help you—eh?

MISS TESMAN (*While he does so*):   How sweet of you! This is just like the old days when you were still with us!

TESMAN (*He turns the hat around in his hands, looking at it admiringly from all sides*):   That's a very elegant hat you've treated yourself to.

MISS TESMAN: I bought that on Hedda's account.

TESMAN: On Hedda's account—eh?

MISS TESMAN: Yes—I didn't want her to feel ashamed of her old aunt—in case we should happen to go out together.

TESMAN (*Patting her cheek*):   What a dear you are, Aunt Juliane—always thinking of everything! (*Puts the hat down on a chair near the table*) And now let's sit down here on

the sofa and have a cozy little chat till Hedda comes.
(*They sit down.* . .)[8]

Actors would appreciate this passage as a perfectly or-
ganic movement that enables them to inhabit their
characters fully. Before dealing with this virtue, however, we should note that here, in this small slice of dialogue, we are in the distinctive presence of *a play* which,
even in its quiet moments, flows constantly on the current of an action. What characterizes this thoroughly
"natural" conversation is its quality of ominous innocence. It does not seem to know that it is significant,
that its words are exactly sufficient to produce what
will follow, that it contains a precise future that will
depend, for example, on the purchase of this fine, elegant hat yesterday, or last week, and put on this chair
today. Yet this is what is known to us as privileged out-
siders; it is not known by our knowing the play in advance but by our knowing that everything in a play
leads, directionally, to the emergence of a subject
which, as it collects more and more history, will become narrower and narrower in focus until it is dis-
charged—in this case in the crack of a pistol, shortly to
be introduced with the same innocence as the hat. Up
to a point a play is a series of givens, in the sense that
givens, appearing ex nihilo, are gratuitously posited
(like Aunt Juliane and her hat); then the givens become
receiveds, that is to say the established and limited al-
phabet with which the play *must* write its unfolding in-
scription. Thus the arbitrary is gradually converted

8. Henrik Ibsen, *Six Plays by Henrik Ibsen,* trans. Eva Le Gallienne (New York: Modern Library, 1957), pp. 346–47.

into the inevitable, and thus the impression of a highly critical causality arises, not especially from the flow of prominent events—A insults B, B slaps A, they duel—but from the accretion of seeming incidentals ("On Hedda's account—eh?") or seeming irrelevancies ("*Puts the hat down on a chair. . .*") that constitutes a closed field of force and creates the illusion of a world whose every detail is temporally and spatially linked: in short, a world permeated with causality.

But it is a world whose causality has been determined in advance by the medium itself. This sequence of words, born on the gesture of the passing hat, is critically tailored to evolve the scene at the speed of the actors' natural rhythm. There is no fat in it; it does not dwell in any of its parts, as a narrative account of the same action might: "Tesman knew that the hat was brand new and that Aunt Juliane would be pleased if he noticed it. Then, suddenly seeing her uncovered head, he thought, 'My goodness, how old she is getting!' . . ." An actor might have such thoughts by way of projecting his attitude about Aunt Juliane; the point is that attitude and action would be inseparable on the stage, whereas in a novel they would be presented sequentially in the word-flow. The expository lag of prose fiction—that is, the narrator's privileged explanation of the action—is made possible by the virtual invisibility of the verbal medium which may interrupt the causal flow at will. The difference between theater's causal flow and the novel's is primarily one of the range and mobility of the narrative eye (a factor that puts the novel close to film). One can argue, for example, that Tolstoi's essays on history are an important part of the causal flow of *War and Peace,* as the essay on cetology is in *Moby Dick*. That is, it is part of the liberty of the novel form to put perspectives on top of perspectives, to reach out in philosophical, biographical, societal, and, most commonly, descriptive directions that lie behind the scene and the action. From the dramatic point of view, these are delays, but from the narrative, or thematic, viewpoint they are enrichments of the novel's projection of its universe. It is exactly because the novel is not fastened *in* the world that it can take virtually anything in the world as its subject. Thus the reading of a novel is a continual act of suspension of some part of the scene or action while another is being developed (as Aunt Juliana is "put on hold" in the mind's eye while we read Tesman's interior monologue in my novelistic revision of the scene). In the theater the "on hold" principle occurs as a visual phenomenon: we simply concentrate our attention on the action (usually a speaking or moving character) and consign the rest of the stage to our peripheral vision where it exerts a pictorial influence, fading, so to speak, into the setting. Most things, particularly motionless things, fade quite easily into the periphery, but the human body quickly becomes *de trop* if it isn't being used. Sleeping or reading a newspaper are forms of use, of course, because they are things characters tend to do; but we have all sensed the discomfort or artificiality of actors who have been asked to "freeze" or to chat inaudibly in party scenes while others occupy our attention downstage. Some of this we readily accept as theatrical convention, but what makes such characters conspicuous is that they are trying so hard not to be conspicuous in a space where the human body cannot easily de-emphasize its presence. This is a principle that O'Neill violated, unsuccessfully, when he asked that characters freeze during the long "thought" speeches of *Strange Interlude*.

It is important to rescue from self-evidence the fact that the actor has only natural equipment. He is the same as any member of the audience. This is the point of departure for his art, which is, paradoxically, the art of doing artificially what everyone else does naturally. This fact of starting always from nothing—an ordinary self—and becoming, say, Othello is the seat of our fascination with the actor. Everything he does is at once an imitation of an action and an action in itself; it is both artificial and natural, both calculated and effortless. We have all sat in the theater and marveled at the power of a single gesture, of an expression of surprise, that would have passed unnoticed in a living room but in the theater takes one's breath away. How is it that such a small event can be so astonishing? It is, of course, the act of control and economy: we all know that it is not easy to be surprised on cue and that the actor, presumably, spends much of his life observing how we express surprise, lift coffee cups, and grow old. But beyond these marks of genius we come back finally to the fact that the surprise was the single and uncontaminated center of everything taking place on the stage at that instant. It occurred at precisely the right moment ("timing") and at the right pitch ("delivery"); it was precisely clear enough to command our attention and natural enough to be seen as having escaped unintentionally from the character's interior. It was a perfect balance of nature and art.

This brings us to the subject of gesture. Semioticians think of gesture as one of two kinds of language the actor uses. This makes sense, if for no other reason than that speech and gesture can be distinguished and have, since classical times, been treated as separate and complementary arts. Othello would naturally accompany the line, "Keep up your bright swords, for the dew will rust them," with a complementary movement (*keep up*) of his arm; or, if the actor chose not to move his arm, that too would be a gesture signifying Othello's perfect confidence in the power of his voice and presence. But phenomenally one would perceive here only a single aural-visual event. It would not be a question of two languages coming together into a unity but of a single *motive* pervading the actor's body and producing speech and movement which, so to speak, collapse into the body of Othello's character. Phenomenologically, gesture must finally be understood not as the kinetic imprint that speech or thought make on the actor's body, or even as something that reflexively precedes speech, as it may, on one level, be argued. Gesture is the *process* of revelation of the actor's presence—in view of our earlier discussion one might say of his "usefulness"—and this presence, as the organ that feeds on the dramatic text, is the governing center of what is possible in the theater. Gesture cannot even be defined as significant visible movement. It no more excludes immobility than speech excludes silence. And all of the texts on chironomy and stage movement are essentially engineering manuals to the basic biophysics text of the actor's corporeality, or presence. We may define gesture as any form of expressiveness in which the actor's body is justified.

Since the importance of this definition is more apparent in the breach than in the observance, let me illustrate it with a play text, or a piece of one, that violates it. It must be said, in preface, that any text, even the text of a phone directory or a soup recipe, could be made lively by a good actor if he can convert it into a kind of plot. Here I am trying to find a text that does not *need* the actor. The one I have in mind—Bryon's *Manfred*—makes no pretention to being a stage play. It is, in fact, a dramatic poem. But my purpose is not to kidnap it from its own domain and torment it in another, but to see why it is a dramatic poem and not a poetic drama. What gets in the way in this soliloquy, in fact, is its very quality as poetry. Since the speech goes on for fifty-six lines, I will quote only enough to suggest the drift of its deficiency as an acting play.

> The spirits I have raised abandon me,
> The spells which I have studied baffle me,
> The remedy I reck'd of tortured me;
> I lean no more on superhuman aid;
> It hath no power upon the past, and for
> The future, till the past be gulf'd in darkness,
> It is not of my search.—My mother Earth!
> And thou fresh breaking Day, and you, ye Mountains,
> Why are ye beautiful? I cannot love ye.
> And thou, the bright eye of the universe,
> That openest over all, and unto all
> Art a delight—thou shin'st not on my heart.
> And you, ye crags, upon whose extreme edge
> I stand, and on the torrent's brink beneath
> Behold the tall pines dwindled as to shrubs
> In dizziness of distance; when a leap,
> A stir, a motion, even a breath, would bring
> My breast upon its rocky bosom's bed
> To rest for ever—wherefore do I pause?

> I feel the impulse—yet I do not plunge;
> I see the peril—yet do not recede;
> And my brain reels—and yet my foot is firm:
> There is a power upon me which withholds,
> And makes it my fatality to live—
>
> *(I, ii, 1–24)*

Of course there is no way to prove that this speech is deficient as drama. One either feels it or not. Moreover, it is possible that the speech, just as it is, could become fully dramatic if it were put into a different context. For example, there is a strong resemblance between Manfred's voice and the voice we hear in certain monologues of Richard II:

>   I weep for joy
> To stand upon my kingdom once again.
> Dear earth, I do salute thee with my hand,
> Though rebels wound thee with their horses' hoofs.
> As a long-parted mother with her child
> Plays fondly with her tears and smiles in meeting,
> So, weeping, smiling, greet I thee, my earth . . .
>
> *(III, ii, 4–10)*

Apart from specific hallmarks of style, the chief difference between Manfred's laments and Richard's is that Richard's rarely constitute the single focus of our attention. They are usually framed in the gathering of an embarrassed court, or, as here, an army watching its leadership dissolve before its eyes. In short, the drama of this most "poetic" of Shakespeare's serious plays is that of a king who plays Manfred while the tide of events sweeps him ever closer to disaster. Still, it is relevant that much of the commentary on this play worries the point I would make, without qualification, about Bryon's *Manfred:* it is basically an exercise in lyric, and what is primarily deficient about the lyric, as drama, is the ratio of words to gestural change. Manfred may be in terrible distress of soul throughout this monologue, but his soul has, so to speak, made up its mind at the beginning. It is lost to the world. The speech elaborates a state of being rather than a process of becoming or a debate of the mind with the soul (as in Hamlet's "To be or not to be . . ."). It reminds one of a physician listing the symptoms of his own fatal disease, almost as an observer who is beyond the pain. And the result is that in all this agitation there is a center of complete calm, the calm of the lyric voice speaking from its poetic sinecure beyond the realm of action. A skillful actor might find ways to lend Manfred a gestural liveliness throughout this speech, but I suspect he would find it difficult to overcome the feeling that he was inventing excuses for the speech and that his body was the superfluous appendage of a voice painting pictures for the ear.

I am not arguing that the lyric voice has no business on the dramatic stage, and the obvious proof that it does would be the Greek tragic chorus. But Greek lyricism is different from romantic lyricism. For one thing, with the exception (chiefly) of certain Euripidean odes, it always presents the communal *effect* of the change that is occurring in the episodes. For another, it is primarily spectacular rather than psychological, and as such lyric voice is the formal element that puts Greek tragedy closer to the tolerances of opera than to those of drama. Our theater bravely attempts Greek tragedy, partly out of a sense of duty and challenge, and partly because we cannot tolerate the idea that such a monumental art form could be beyond our powers. But the fact remains that we cannot dissolve the expectations born of thousands of realistic and deterministic plays. We are at a complete loss when it comes to the chorus. We trim it, divide it into subgroups, and naturalize it, and the more we do so the more awkward it becomes. It is not that our actors cannot sing or dance or chant; rather, it is that something archaic in the lyrical content of the chorus will not translate into a convincing gestural presence. It is impossible for the modern actor to stand, history-less, at that naive point in time when the dramatic principle had just begun to isolate itself from the lyric and epic principles. Add to this that the theogonic music of the chorus is even further removed from possible embodiment by the absurdity of a modern translation. One is often reminded of those old Westerns in which the Indians were played by a congeries of extras who had the city written all over their faces.

The task of the dramatist, then, is to offer the actor a text with which he can perform his unique service—to be fully present, to change before our eyes, even if the change consists in remaining himself at all times. The boring actor is one whose gestural and vocal equipment performs the different tasks of his role in the same way. Our unconscious demand that there be something constantly *emergent* in the actor's performance is nowhere better illustrated than in the theatrical criticism of the great actors, which is substantially a descriptive history of how well the actor gets from one moment to another or from one role to another. For instance, Hazlitt on Edmund Kean's Hamlet: "His surprise when he first sees the Ghost, his eagerness and filial confidence in following it, the impressive pathos of his action and voice in addressing it, 'I'll call thee Hamlet, Father, Royal Dane,' were admirable."[9]

There is one other aspect of the actor's influence on the dramatic text that we should take up before turning to the actor/audience relationship. If character and event meet in the actor, it follows that every trait of every character in a play must make its special contribution to the action. This amounts to saying that every character trait is an event in the plot. For one cannot get very far into the causal origin of an event in a play — say, Hamlet stabbing Polonius — without seeing that it is made of motives and motives are made of traits. Or, to put it another way, if your psychological portrait of Hamlet contains such and such a trait (impulsiveness, rashness), it was determined by what Hamlet has impulsively done, not by some general trait of impulsiveness in his nature. One might conceivably say this of literary character as well (depending on how one defined a literary event); but there is no generic basis on which one can distinguish literary and dramatic (and, by extension, theatrical) character as separate species of behavior. The only restriction on the novelist's material is that it be narratable, and narratability happens to include, as one of its many possibilities, everything that

9. William Hazlitt, *Hazlitt on Theatre,* eds. William Archer and Robert Lowe (New York: Hill and Wang, n.d.), p. 13.

can be staged. Thus literary or narrated character over-laps dramatic character and becomes potentially theatrical to the extent that it reveals itself in performable behavior. On this ground many novels have provided the material for successful plays. Beckett, who is a playwright, does not (for the most part) write such novels; Dostoevsky, who was not a playwright, did, and entire scenes from his novels can be performed on stage by simply converting the description into stage directions. In short, what the dramatist *must* do as a condition of his medium, the novelist *may* do if his project (or his imagination) requires it.

To extend our actor / character principle a step further, we might liken a character's traits to the physical properties of a substance. In fact, let us borrow a precept from the theory of causality: "Therefore every substance," Kant says in *The Critique of Pure Reason*, "must contain in itself the causality of certain determinations in another substance, and, at the same time, the effects of the causality of that other substance, that is, substances must stand in dynamical communion, immediately or mediately, with each other, if their coexistence is to be known in any possible experience."[10] We are not concerned here with how correctly Kant's proposition describes the world of matter but only with the metaphorical value it may have for helping us to understand the "substance" of dramatic character. Here, surely, is a theatrical view of the universe, rather than a novelistic view. By this I mean that one might think of a play as a closed society of "substances" coexisting in

10. Immanuel Kant, *Critique of Pure Reason*, trans. F. Max Müller (Garden City, N.Y.: Doubleday, 1961), p. 146.

"dynamical communion." These substances of course are characters represented by actors; and everything we have said about the actor suggests the respect in which the requirements posed by his physical being differentiate dramatic texts, in degree if not in kind, from all others. Thus through Kant's proposition we might convert Aristotle's "imitation of an action" into the imitation of *causality*—not, certainly, by way of improving it, but by way of bringing action, act-er (character), and actor together as the final, formal, and material causes of drama.

One way to illustrate how the principle of causality works in the drama is to imagine a play as a mechanical model that performs one task. The simplest is probably the proverbial row of dominoes set on end. The dramatic feature here is the shackling of independent events in an interlocking sequence with a beginning, a middle, and an end. The first event leads by probability or necessity to the last. This may be amusing to watch on a card table, but it would make a monotonous plot. Things become more interesting—that is, more dramatic—if we graduate to billiard balls placed in a "random" formation on the table, and in one strike of the cue we provoke an action that knocks them all, eventually, into the pockets. The improvement over the domino plot lies in the fact that each ball seems to have an independent career, or *character,* when set in motion, yet its career is precisely the causal factor in the demise of another ball. In other words, this plot is not simply a straightforward action: it offers the torqued evolution of a reversal as well. But however much the intricacy of this model resembles a Feydeau farce or the last act of a Jacobean tragedy, the most important resemblance to drama lies in the closed field of force itself. The interest, as in a play, arises from the fact that we begin with a given number of elements and we use them up as efficiently as possible. In this respect, the cast of characters on the program of any play announces the ingredients in the play's forthcoming feat of efficient demolition. For example: Deeley, Anna, and Kate in Pinter's *Old Times*. There is something brash—unlike the dinner menu—in the program's confidence in our interest in these people (Deeley *who?*). Yet sitting in the theater, anticipating this new play by Harold Pinter, one knows that this trio of characters, played by X, Y, and Z, constitutes a field of emotional energy different from anything to be found in the open world. The phenomenal message of the cast list, in fact, is that it predicts a future that has already been secured, like the inevitable paths of motion in the randomly placed billiard balls. These three people are posited as being about to exist and, as the curtain rises, as having existed ("all in their early forties"); but their existence is confined to the single action that binds them together in what the Elizabethans called "the argument." However real they seem to be, through the reality of the actors, they have only one drama—two hours of life—and it will be successfully concluded when they have used each other up, as in a game of giveaway checkers. This implies no reference to the emotional violence in the play itself but only to the efficiency of dramatic character in which nothing is left over, not a hint of independent liveliness, that is not consumed in action—or, to retain the sense of family intimacy, in *inter*action.

Thus plays, in their fashion, are efficient machines whose parts are characters who are made of actors. All characters in a play are nested together in "dynamical communion," or in what we might call a reciprocating balance of nature: every character "contains in itself" the *cause* of actions, or determinations, in other characters and the effects of their causality. (Dialogue, by this token, is a continuous oscillation of cause and effect: each line is the *effect* of the preceding line and the *cause* of the line to follow.) And, as in the physical world, if a character's properties are altered his place in the play's nature is altered as well.

Let us see more specifically how this might work by altering some of the more important properties of characters in *Hamlet*. If we think away from Claudius's character a certain trait of public likability, coupled with a visible political competence, the play's chemistry is instantly unbalanced. For one thing, we throw the whole issue of Hamlet's behavior onto a problematical level. If Claudius were, let us say, like Don John, a plain-dealing villain for all to see, we would shortly begin questioning Hamlet's introspections and self-doubts. We would soon become impatient and wonder what in the world was holding him back; and all of Hamlet's good qualities, among which we would number his piercing intelligence, would be stained by the absurdity of his neglect. It would be absolutely comic to see him walk on stage reading a book. As Claudius is portrayed, however, Shakespeare has finely tuned him to be something of an enigma, and hence a dramaturgical motive for Hamlet's delay. He is a man who has, in fact, committed a vile crime, but he does not behave like a criminal for most of the play, not even when he is alone with his own thoughts (the "prayer" scene, in this sense, is a mediate way of delaying Hamlet's revenge on purely dynamical grounds). This does not account for why Hamlet does not dispatch Claudius posthaste, but it prevents us from worrying too much why he doesn't. *We* can understand why Hamlet might have scruples about killing him, even though Hamlet doesn't! Or, if we think away from Gertrude's character a certain vagueness, we complicate Hamlet's problem (and the play's) in still another direction. The dramatic need to keep Hamlet away from his mother until the right time, when all the floodgates could be broken at once, was obviously on Shakespeare's mind when he has the Ghost tell Hamlet to "leave her to heaven"—that is, leave her to act 4; and Shakespeare has backed up this command with a Gertrude personality that does not contain the answer to the obvious question: How involved *was* she in the events preceding the play? Hamlet's accusation in the bedroom scene may cleave her heart in twain and turn her eyes into her very soul where she sees "such black and grained spots / As will not leave their tinct," but only Gertrude, alas, knows what these spots may refer to.

What we learn from such tinkering with a play's chemical balance is that its characters form a sort of bootstrap universe that pulls itself into coexistence like the self-drawing hands in Escher's lithograph. Hamlet is made of Gertrude and Claudius, Osric and Horatio, Rosencrantz and Guildenstern, et cetera and vice versa. Seen from the characterological viewpoint, Hamlet is a collection of relationships. The feeling we have that a character in a play is portable and adaptable to other relationships is an illusion born of his resemblance to a human being. In this vein, it has always been a popular critical sport to lift Shakespeare's heroes out of their proper plays and put them in others. Thus it runs that if Hamlet were in Othello's place he would have seen through Iago as quickly as he sees through Rosencrantz and Guildenstern. Othello wouldn't be caught dead murdering Duncan for his throne, and Macbeth, in Hamlet's place, would have "unseam'd" his king early in act 2. But if one looks more closely one discovers that these are largely empty hypotheses, like the notion that Shakespeare's heroines had girlhoods. Removing a character from a play is like trying to pull up an oak tree: much of the soil of the play comes with him. Apart from his given acts and relationships, a character will not translate into a foreign situation. Yet we recall that Hamlet is our modern archetypal hero, above all other heroes in Shakespeare. Mallarmé even coined a syndrome called *Hamletism*. But it isn't Hamlet's character, as something that can be adjusted to fit into different kinds of situations, that constitutes *Hamletism*. It is rather a certain relational equation, or closed field, between man and the world, or between a capacity and a demand. When Coleridge confessed his own likeness to Hamlet ("I have a smack of Hamlet myself, if I may say so"), he was referring to the prevalance in himself of "the abstracting and generalizing habit over the practical."[11] In other words, in order to have a Hamlet, or even a smack of one, one must have a Claudius as well—that is, a condition in the world that must be redressed by practical action.[12]

11. Samuel Taylor Coleridge, *Coleridge's Writings on Shakespeare,* ed. Terence Hawkes (New York: Capricorn Books, 1959), p. 140.
12. A possible exception to this argument might be the so-called stock character, or stereotype, who, as the history of drama will show, seems infinitely portable. Theophrastus's book of *The Char-*

What we mean, partially, by saying that a play is a closed field is that everything faces in toward a center. On the level of locale, this is the place represented by the stage to which everything comes. On the level of characterization the closed field implies a principle we might refer to as *directional lifelikeness*: every character shows only its contributory side. But at the same time the fact that it doesn't have another side escapes us because lifelikeness is always complete no matter how little of it we can see. Leonardo's sketch of the man's foot is no less "real" because it is not attached to the man. Osric is just as lifelike as Hamlet: if his philosophy is thin there is nothing in the least thin about his dimensionality. What shows of his character is exactly enough to admit him fully into *Hamlet*'s world to per-

---

acters is a description of thirty such types. The method consists primarily of defining a character trait ("Arrogance is the habit of despising everybody except oneself") and then illustrating how a man dominated by that trait would behave in a dozen or so situations ("The arrogant man is one who will say, to someone who is in a hurry to speak with him, that he will see him after dinner when he takes his walk") (*The Characters and Menander Plays and Fragments,* trans. Philip Vellacott [Baltimore: Penguin Books, 1967], p. 48). Among Shakespeare's minor characters, Osric might be considered as a combination of two compatible Theophrastus types, the chatterer and the ingratiating man—and you can imagine any number of situations in business, at court, at the concert hall, on a country outing, or on a ship voyage in which Osric would play the candy-tongued and crook-kneed courtier to the hilt. But of course we haven't really lifted Osric out of his situation; we have simply put him back into the same situation over and again. We have changed the scenery, not the plot. You can't possibly imagine how Osric would behave if he were called upon to murder his uncle—unless you could somehow convert such a summons into a comic occasion for chattering and ingratiation.

form his appointed task of negotiating the duel in which Hamlet is slain. Thus we make the same perceptual inference about the stage character as we make about the locale: beyond this wall, painted on the canvas surface, are other rooms, and beyond this house there are streets and other houses, and so on. When a character leaves the stage we think of him as going elsewhere in the same world. In the wings, he continues to live in the dotted-line realm of etcetera behavior, moving (if we happen to think of him at all) more or less at that same momentum that took him out of the play.

In other words, we real-ize the characters of a play just as we tend to fictionalize the people in our lives. That is, we grant characters in a play a peripheral life they do not have, and we see people as characters in the closed field of our own life. We know most people only directionally, in one context—as clerk, customer, teacher, dentist, bus companion, and so on. They play roles in our life (and of course we play roles in theirs).[13] And though we do not suppose that they cease to exist when we part company, or that they go on doing the same thing, it is always astonishing to see them out of context, to see our dentist, for example, on vacation without the props (drill and chair) of his contribution to our life. What makes this astonishing is our sense of always being at the center of the world. It is impossible to escape the feeling that the world is *there for us,* or

13. On the general subject of role playing and its relevance to theater and to life, see Bruce Wilshire's excellent *Role Playing and Identity: The Limits of Theatre as Metaphor* (Bloomington: Indiana University Press, 1982). I might add that Wilshire's book offers a thorough clarification of what is entailed in a phenomenological approach to theater, far more so than my own.

against us (in the case of the paranoic), but always a circumference with our consciousness at its center. In this personal sense, it is not true that "one man in his time plays many parts": he is the protagonist of a life that resembles a play in the persistence of its subject. Each of us regards our own history from the perspective of a self that has survived it, and in this fact is lodged the whole mystery of time and memory. All of this is condensed, miraculously, into the two-hour traffic of a play. The thing we call our *self*—the "I" that is always speaking, the eye that is always perceiving—has its analogue in the drama in the fact that Hamlet is always Hamlet. The deep creatural sympathy we feel for Hamlet arises from the fact that the man who says, "The rest is silence," is the same man who a little earlier (three hours by the theater clock) said, " A little more than kin and less than kind." These are Hamlet's first and last words. In the interim we have essentially been through a whole life. We have, as we say, empathized with Hamlet—by which we mean that Hamlet's history has been the interim project in which the attention of our senses has been consumed. We have lived another life, peculiarly inserted into our own here and now, which has produced the effect of an entelechial completion, dimly like the effect of an out-of-body experience in which we are presumably able to see ourselves from an impossible perspective.

For the fundamental power of this image of "another life" is that we do *oversee* it as we live it empathically. In this respect, I would differentiate the power of theater and the power of film: film envelops us and puts us into its world more or less as we are visually within our own. In this, film and prose fiction are similar: they give us, by different means, the illusion of an unmediated experience. For this reason I suppose most people think of their lives—if they have reveries in this vein at all—as being like films and novels rather than plays. These are the media, at once intimate and spacious, with almost unlimited power to imitate our experience of being present in the world: the daily texture of life, the "aroundness" of space, the continuity (or the return or the lapse) of time, above all the shape we think of our life as accumulating (its crises, its ups and downs, its chapters, the slow composition of its destiny), all given the dignity of significance by an imaginary orchestra or a sympathetic narrator (oneself, of course) who understands everything about us that the world has misunderstood.

This is not the sort of "other life" offered by the play. We are more apt to say that an evening or an experience was like a play (people "create scenes" in restaurants, at parties, etc.). Obviously, I am making no categorical claims about the limits of film, fiction, and drama, or what they can or should do. Plays may very effectively imitate whole lives, some good examples being *Tamburlaine, Peer Gynt,* and *Krapp's Last Tape* (in its own ingenious way); and films regularly invade the dramatic province for their plots. I mean, simply, to isolate characteristics of the forms that encourage certain kinds of fiction and degrees of illusionary involvement. Theater, especially since the advent of the novel, is by and large the form designed for the brief chronicle: *the* crisis, *the* turning point, *the* consequence of the act or the non-act. Theater is swift (even Chekhov is swift). This swiftness has nothing to do with clock time or the suspense of the plot, but only with the fact that *everything*

happens through the actor. This is the swiftness of condensation, of life raised to an intense power of temporal
and spatial density. It is evinced in what Kierkegaard
calls the actor's "elemental tirelessness" that "only hints
at how much more [he] possesses," and, again, in the
"prodigious burden" of his having "to support the illusion of the stage and the weight of everyone's eyes."[14]
Because the theater has so few powers to arrest the attention of the spectator (on milieu or fantasy, for example), its métier is what best divulges its artifice: the intensity of its speech (poetry in a film, unless the poetry
of a parent play, would be unimaginable), the muscu-
larity of its tableaux, its frugal manipulation of empirical time and place—all of those things, in short, that
tainted film in the early days when it thought of itself as
a new form of theater. Thus one witnesses a play as an
event in the real world as well as an illusion of an unreal
world, and its realism is not simply the descriptive realism of either cinema or fiction but the weakly disguised
reality of the actor and the raised platform on which he
stands. The intimacy of theater is not the intimacy of
being within its world but of being present at its
world's origination under all the constraints, visible
and invisible, of immediate actuality.

Consider, as an extraordinary symptom of all this,
two legendary facts from the history of theater: Molière
and Kean were stricken in performance and died soon
after. One always hears these events recited with a certain awe and pride, as though they held a mysterious justice (not moral, of course, but occupational) or a charm-
ing symmetry (Molière, of all things, was playing his

14. Kierkegaard, *Crisis in the Life of an Actress,* pp. 74, 77.

hypochondriac!). But surely we can go deeper. There is, after all, little such fascination in a race driver's dying behind the wheel (where else?). I think the fascination takes us to the very core of the theater experience: on the one hand, how impertinent of nature to shatter the illusion of art, to touch these two men when they were not, so to speak, themselves; on the other, it was precisely the strain of the illusion that brought nature into play.[15] But the fascination of a stricken Kean or Molière does not arise simply from the fact that they were energetically impersonating characters. Had Molière collapsed in rehearsal, the event would lose its phenomenal significance and become a detail in his obituary. The mystery rests, rather, in the fact that the event took place in the theater under the weight of all those eyes. Surely here, of all places, Molière should be guaranteed a temporary immunity to the laws of nature, somewhat like a criminal in the sanctuary of a church. What creates the illusion of such a guarantee, of course, is that the theater tells only marvelous lies. Here there is the absolute certainty of a beginning, a middle, and an end, an orderly arrangement of parts, a certain magnitude ("for beauty," as Aristotle says, "depends on magnitude")—in short, the concentrated destiny of those who are marked out for good or bad fortune, brought about "contrary to expectation, yet logically." This much, at least, is far from life, which is lived in the mean regions of high probability:

15. Of course, nature had been "touching" both actors for some time in the form of advanced tuberculosis, aggravated, in Kean's case, by a style of living that was at least as exhausting as performance itself. Kean did not die until the summer of 1833, almost two months after his final performance in *Othello* at Covent Garden.

normal events, unevents, subliminally (even) disap-
pointments. Thus this sudden closure of art and nature
on the evening of February 17, 1673, constituted an
abrupt reversal in the theatrical roles of imagery and actuality, or (if you will) figure and ground. Nature, "recursively" imbedded in the illusion, was improvising
her own play-within-a-play in which Molière, like the
Roman actor in Massinger's tragedy, was enacting his
own death.[16]

16. I use the word *recursively* strictly in Douglas Hofstadter's definition in *Gödel, Escher, Bach: An Eternal Golden Braid* (New York: Random House, 1980): "A *recursive* figure is one whose ground can be
seen as a figure in its own right" (p. 67). The idea I am aiming at is
that the actor's body, normally perceived as the "ground" of the stage
figure, suddenly becomes a figure "in its own right."

5

Actor / Audience

I will not dwell much on audience response as an influential factor in the actor's performance: its laughter in comedy, the overflow of feeling in its silence in tragedy, the effects of group apathy or approval on the vulnerable actor—overall, the implied speech behind its attention, the weight of its eyes. Beneath these considerations is a more elementary one from which they all derive. As I suggested earlier, there is a deeply ritualistic vestige in the theater experience. We like to trace this back to primitive ritual (being, as Nietzsche says, bereft of myth ourselves), back to the enactment of the conflict among gods or of the scriptures, or to the imitation of the seasonal and natural cycles. Whatever the historical validity of this idea, the ritual basis of theater has little to do with memory traces of early man. It would be more reasonable to say that theater and primitive ritual, however different in social function, share an energy and structure that one can detect in the Wednesday evening play-reading group as easily as one can in the enactment of the Passion in the Easter service. The ritual in theater is based in the community's need for *the thing* that transpires in theater and in the designation, or self-designation, of certain individuals who, for one reason or another, consent to become the embodiment of this thing. The fact that this may be pleasurable or ego satisfying for such individuals is not as important as that theater is a license for a remarkable exercise in group imagination. Rousseau was right in coupling theater and the public forum as the only places which unite spectacle and discourse. But, for personal reasons, he was unable to see theater as a natural complement to the forum in that the actor, like the orator, also speaks for himself to the community, but he speaks in a different language.

Aristotle says that imitation is "congenital to human beings from childhood," and neo-Aristotelians like Francis Fergusson point to the play of kittens pretending they are hunters (before there is anything to hunt) as an even more basic form of imitation.[1] But the imitative assertion that one so readily finds in solitary children and kittens somehow atrophies with the formation of the adult personality. It is now seen (through the adult smile) that imitation was a way of learning how to become an adult. There is something about the imitation of another human being, about speaking in another's voice, that requires either a creatural naiveté, a touch of madness, or an invited audience. If my neighbor beyond our shared fence hears me singing "Thy Tiny Hand is Frozen," he will certainly be amused, but probably no more surprised than if he had peered over the fence to find me sketching my cat asleep under the tree. But if he overheard me reciting Brutus's "It must be by his death" soliloquy, he might think about calling the police or the hospital. Why are we so astounded by the adult who impersonates for an audience consisting of himself? Why do we feel only humor, or good feeling, when we hear someone break into song in the shower or on a public street? The distance between song and impersonation is

1. Fergusson, *The Idea of a Theater,* p. 251.

obvious. Song is only the expression of emotion; or it may be that melody is simply pleasurable in itself and that when we want to hear a particular melody we become the instrument of our own pleasure, a kind of natural radio. Song is lyrical: the whole body may feel the power of song and, carried far enough in the direction of the dithyramb (as in rock music), may even become possessed by song. But within the normal range, song does not affect identity. It is like laughter or weeping: it simply alters the composure of identity.

But the solitary actor is a suspicious fellow. He has somehow violated the norm of behavior we call "being oneself." To encounter someone acting is, as Sartre puts it, to encounter someone "devoured by the imaginary."[2] And Plato was among the earliest critics of acting to point out the kinship of this unreal state to madness. On the stage, however, the solitary actor is absolved of the charge of derangement. Here it is permissible to be devoured by the imaginary because it becomes an act of speech, as opposed to an unexplained subjectivity. Before an audience, in other words, if one imitates a madman one is no longer doubly mad, but mad as Hamlet put it, in craft—mad north-by-northwest. To return to our idea of the actor as a storyteller, the madman becomes the "he," or the character in the world of the play who is always saying "I" and "It hath made me mad." Thus the character is the actor's subject, what he speaks of, the matter between the "I" and the "you" in the aesthetic discourse. The actor invites the audience to look through him at someone else—or, recalling the mirror image, at *itself.*

2. Sartre, *Sartre on Theater,* p. 162.

This idea of theater as an act of speech allows us to see how the actor's relationship to the audience may shift keys during a performance or, on the longer range, as culture makes different demands on the theater as a reflection of its own concerns. In effect, the actor has three pronominal modes in which he may speak to the audience, and they are modes—not styles—that cover all possibilities simply because they are all that discourse contains. Our chart from the preceding chapter would now look like this:

I (actor)	=	Self-expressive mode
You (audience)	=	Collaborative mode
He (character)	=	Representational mode

Before defining and exemplifying these modes I must emphasize that in treating the actor as a speaker I also have in mind the audience as listener. Any speaker-listener relationship is a two-way street, and the listener may hear selectively what he wants to hear or what he thinks he hears. In other words, it is not a simple matter of following the intention of the speaker but of abandoning one's senses to the shifting appeals of the speech (and the actor's speech, of course, should be understood to include gesture, presence, and all the aspects of his performance of the role). Above all, I want to avoid any suggestion that my modes have anything at all to do with style, or necessarily to do with sudden and conscious shifts in the actor's deportment whereby we now perceive him in one mode of listening and now in another. I am interested only in trying to approximate the range of the actor / audience relationship; and it is simply not sufficient to say that the actor performs in various styles (declamatory, naturalistic, romantic, estranged, etc.) or, beyond style, that the audience's perception of the actor is exhausted in his dual nature as actor and character. But I can make this clear only by examining the modes themselves.

Let us begin by treating them as pure modes of performance. In the self-expressive mode the actor seems to be performing on his own behalf. He says, in effect, "See what I can do." One might say that certain roles encourage the self-expressive tendency (Cyrano, Faust, Falstaff, Hamlet, Lear, Medea), either because they are so demanding or because they have been deliberately designed as vehicles for the release of the actor's power (the part of Cyrano, for example, was written as a showpiece for Coquelin). Moreover, certain authors (usually the classic poets of the art) encourage the self-expressive mode. There is no better way to illustrate this idea than to quote Hazlitt on the occasion of Kean's appearance in *Richard II* in 1815:

It may be asked, then, why all great actors choose characters from Shakespeare to come out in; and again, why these become their favourite parts? First, it is not that they are able to exhibit their author, but that he enables them to show themselves off. The only way in which Shakespeare appears to greater advantage on the stage than common writers is, that he stimulates the faculties of the actor more. If he is a sensible man, he perceives how much he has to do, the inequalities he has to contend with, and he exerts himself accordingly; he puts himself at full speed, and lays all his resources under contribution; he attempts more, and makes a greater number of brilliant failures; he does all he can, and bad is often the best.[3]

Converting Hazlitt to our own purposes, we might interpret the actor's decision to play big parts like Lear or Richard as a self-expressive act in which he bets the audience that he is actor enough to fill the character's shoes. On its part, the audience goes to the theater to see Kean rather than to see the character Kean is impersonating. I am not suggesting that this is the only motive in playing and playgoing, only that the great classical plays (particularly in the eighteenth and nineteenth century when they are more frequently on the boards) seem to charge the theatrical event with the electricity of competition. In other words, the actor was invited to put himself "at full speed," and to the extent that one went to the theater to see Kean or Macready or Mrs. Siddons at full speed one would be listening in the self-expressive mode.

As another variation, a play might be deliberately converted into a self-expressive vehicle—as in the star system or in the *Hamlet* productions of Charlotte Cushman, Sarah Bernhardt, and Judith Anderson. Certain speeches in plays call for a high degree of self-expressiveness (the opening of *Richard III*, Hotspur's Popinjay speech, Mercutio's Mab speech). In this sense, opera, dance, and mime are the major self-expressive forms of theater. Whatever they are *about* is always less important than what they display. The best-known example is the opera soprano who is not expected to disappear into her role as a dying tubercular, because it is im-

3. Hazlitt, *Hazlitt on Theatre*, p. 51.

possible to sing properly and die properly at the same time. Likewise, in dance, what story we have is there less as an illusion than as a display case for a series of demanding solo variations. The secondary role played by verisimilitude in these forms is confirmed by the fact that the performer often steps completely out of the illusion and bows to the audience's applause when the solo is over. And so with mime, which is essentially an act of defining an invisible world in terms of the visible body. We don't see the walls of Marcel Marceau's prison or the stairs he ascends or the wind he leans into; his body opens onto the structure of these things in a display of the artist's ability to do without them.

In dramatic theater, putting aside the great roles and the great poetic arias, self-expressiveness asserts itself in the form of vignettes, cameo moments, *lazzi,* or, more generally, in the actor's particular stylistic signature: Garrick's kaleidoscope of facial expressions, Edward Alleyn's thunder, Kean's "flashes of lightning," Mrs. Siddons's majesty, Duse's restraint, Bernhardt's Bernhardt, and finally Brando's (then everyone's) realer realism. Veltrusky mentions the passage in *My Life in Art* where Stanislavski talks about the Russian actor, Yermilov Sadovsky, who had a particular piece of business that contains the essence of the actor's self-enlargement of his role: he "suddenly stopped in the middle of a sentence to portray the character feeling in his mouth for a hair from his fur collar, and went on for a long time moving his tongue around and 'trying to take the hair out' with his fingers while the sentence he had begun remained unfinished."[4] What is the interest in this search for a hair?

4. Veltrusky, "Contribution to the Semiotics of Acting," p. 572.

In life it would be unremarkable, if not vulgar; on the stage, it is memorable. It is exactly the revelation of something hitherto subtheatrical, not simply realism but an audacious display of the actor's power to be "real" on the microlevel. In such a moment (assuming it is well done) the qualities Kierkegaard calls "exuberance" and "absolute assurance" come together to form the "playfulness" possessed by the actor of genius. He says, in effect, "Here is the original of your own search for the hair," or, "You have all searched for a hair: let us see, comically, what this search amounts to." I suggest it is the essence of the actor's self-enlargement for another reason: here the sentence the actor is speaking might be said to stand for the conventional flow of theater action; everything is going along as written. But suddenly the flow is broken, a fissure opens, and out pops a new delight, a slice of human behavior that exists, in cameo, for its own sake.

It is not that the actor steps out of character in such moments but that he finds the fissure in the text that allows him to make his unique contribution: he self-creates the real ground of his character's ideality. There was a memorable moment of this kind in the Eva Le Gallienne and Irene Worth production of *Mary Stuart* when Elizabeth held a stare for what seemed like minutes while trying to determine whether Mortimer was a true or a false servant. The idea in the *enacted event* was to arrest Elizabeth's character on the fundamental point of her indecision. The idea in the *acting event,* as Miss Le Gallienne admitted, was to arrest the audience on the point of intense concentration as long as possible. The moment was pure Elizabeth and pure Le Gallienne, and one was left to wonder how it could ever have been done differently. But midway in the stare one felt the pure presence of whatever it is that makes theater, as Diderot said, "a different world."

It is plain that the self-expressive mode cannot be contained in stylistic terms. It is our awareness of the artist in the actor. The rationale for positing such a mode of performance is that there ought to be a word for, or a way of isolating, something as powerful as the pleasure we take when artistry becomes the object of our attention. In opera, dance, and mime the artist is almost constantly this object. In view of theater's strong illusionary mission, the actor is less so: he comes in and out of focus as an artist; now we see the character, now the artist in a moment of genius or, conversely, the unshielded actor in a moment of flaw. But even in theater there are degrees of artist-presence. We always recognize Olivier in Hamlet or Olivier behind the dark paint of Othello. But this is not what is meant by artist-presence; this is simply actor-presence. The distinction is roughly that between *doing* and *being*: when the artist in the actor comes forth we are reacting to the actor's particular way of *doing* his role. Our awareness of the artist is likely to come at certain peaks in a performance when the character given to the actor by the dramatist is endowed with its perfect personality. It is not that the personality is less perfect elsewhere, simply that a character of almost any kind, from Osric to Hamlet, contains countless openings for solo variation. There is always a potential interstice in the text. A character, Diderot says, is an "ideal type." Within the range of a certain typology one can imagine Hamlet doing and being many things that are not written into his character. What a dramatic text offers the actor is an ideal portrait, an abstraction, that can be made real in a thousand ways. To return to our earlier question: what the text of *Hamlet* offers the reader is a full portrait of a man we see in the mind's eye; what it offers the actor is a subject out of which he will create a living portrait with his own original resources.

Let us take two instances from theater history that will dramatize the range of the actor's self-expressiveness. There are actors whose genius rests in the fact that they play themselves. This is not entirely the metaphor it may seem. Kean was obviously such an actor, an idea that Sartre develops very wittily in his play about Kean. Another was Bernhardt, and I can think of no better way to document the self-ostentatious side of the self-expressive mode than to quote Arthur Symons's brilliant description of Bernhardt at work:

The art of Sarah Bernhardt has always been a very conscious art, but it so spoke to us, once, that it was difficult to analyse it coldly. She was Phèdre or Marguerite Gautier, she was Adrienne Lecouvreur, Fédora, La Tosca, the actual woman, and she was also that other actual woman, Sarah Bernhardt. The two magics met and united, in the artist and the woman, each alone of its kind. There was an excitement in going to the theatre; one's pulses beat feverishly before the curtain had risen; there was almost a kind of obscure sensation of peril, such as one feels when the lioness leaps into the cage, on the other side of the bars. And the acting was like a passionate declaration, offered to some one unknown; it was as if the whole nervous force of the audience were sucked out of it and flung back, intensified, upon itself, as it encountered the single, insatiable, indomitable nervous force of the woman. And so, in its way, this very artificial acting seemed the mere instinctive, irresistible expression of a temperament; it mesmerised one, awakening the senses and sending the intelligence to sleep.[5]

5. Arthur Symons, *Eleanora Duse* (New York: Duffield 1927), p. 151.

Who could go to see *Phèdre* or *La Dame aux Camélias* and become lost in the illusion in the presence of this energy? "It is all sheer acting," Symons says. What is it, then, that Bernhardt *does to* the text? Where does she find its interstices?

The first thing one notices in her acting, when one is free to watch it coolly, is the way in which she subordinates effects to effect. She has her crescendos, of course, and it is these which people are most apt to remember, but the extraordinary force of these crescendos comes from the smooth and level manner in which the main part of the speaking is done. She is not anxious to make points at every moment, to put all the possible emphasis into every separate phrase; I have heard her glide over really significant phrases which, taken by themselves, would seem to deserve more consideration, but which she has wisely subordinated to an overpowering effect of ensemble. Sarah Bernhardt's acting reminds me of a musical performance. . . . [She] is always the actress as well as the part; when she is at her best, she is both equally, and our consciousness of the one does not disturb our possession by the other. When she is not at her best, we see only the actress, the incomparable craftswoman openly labouring at her work (pp. 154–55).

On the other end of the same spectrum we find Eleanora Duse who, on occasion, played the same roles as Bernhardt in other theaters of the same city, and nightly she performed only the miracle of her own disappearance. Overall, as a stylist, Duse's acting would best be studied as an example of the third-personal, or representational, mode of performance. But she had her moments, her crescendos, in which the disappearance was so complete that the artist reappeared on the other side of the illusion— that is to say, stunned the audience with the fidelity of the artifice. Shaw relates

such a moment in her performance of Magda in Suder-
mann's *Home*. In the third act Magda must face the unexpected arrival of the father of her child in her own
father's living room. It is a moment of extreme tension
and she (Magda, the character) gets through it "pretty
well," Shaw says. But just when her composure seems
to be returning and she seems safely over the embarrassment and shock

a terrible thing happened to her. She began to blush; and in
another moment she was conscious of it, and the blush was
slowly spreading and deepening until, after a few vain ef-
forts to avert her face or to obstruct his view of it without
seeming to do so, she gave up and hid the blush in her
hands. After that feat of acting I did not need to be told why
Duse does not paint an inch thick. I could detect no trick in
it: it seemed to me a perfectly genuine effect of the dramatic
imagination. In the third act of *La Dame aux Camélias*,
where she produces a touching effect by throwing herself
down, and presently rises with her face changed and flushed
with weeping, the flush is secured by the preliminary
plunge to a stooping attitude, imagination or no imagination; but Magda's blush did not admit of that explanation;
and I must confess to an intense professional curiosity as to
whether it always comes spontaneously.[6]

What occurs to one while reading these two reports
of great moments in the theater is the marvel of our
sensitivity to that zone of behavior within which the act
of acting takes place. To recognize the natural progress
of a blush as a "feat of acting" one must be able to hold

    6. George Bernard Shaw, *Our Theatres in The Nineties*, vol. 3 of
Collected Works, Ayot St. Lawrence ed. (New York: W. H. Wise,
1931), p. 162.

in mind two categories—that of the real and that of the imaginary—that are fused in a single phenomenon. How does one see it as art when the art consists precisely in making it real? Of course Shaw is hardly an average theatergoer, but surely he is describing something about Duse that brought audiences to the theater to see her. In fact, here we have a direct window into "the end of playing": Duse does not fool us into taking her for Magda any more than Bernhardt, for the simple reason that a theater is not a palace of illusion. Sartre puts it neatly: The actor "draws his pride in the fact that he would not be admired for 'being' the character so well unless everyone, starting precisely with himself, knew that he was not."[7] So we do see style at all times; it simply emerges more beautifully at certain times than others. Symons and Shaw were stunned by Bernhardt and Duse. They are both great actresses not because they draw us perceptually into the imaginary but because they present the real in nearly pure form, the fictions of Magda and Phèdre being a means to this end. It would be wrong, of course, to dismiss the imaginary element of performance, and it is true that both Symons and Shaw could as easily have written about the characters being played by Bernhardt and Duse without reference to the means through which they were communicated. But, as it happens, they were describing the art in the actress and how it exists as the object of our attention: Duse quietly hides herself in the character; Bernhardt converts the character into "the expression of a temperament." In Duse's case, the wonder is that the woman understood the character so well and could force her soul so much to her own conceit

7. Sartre, *Sartre on Theater,* pp. 165–166.

that she could become the woman she played without, so to speak, selling her soul in the process. In Bernhardt's case the wonder is that the woman could elevate artificiality ("sheer acting") to such an intense level that she herself could devour the imaginary and "substitute" herself (as Shaw says) for the character.

I would prefer a less clumsy term than collaborative for the second personal mode of performance, but it suggests the main idea: to break down the distance between actor and audience and to give the spectator something more than a passive role in the theater exchange. The invitation to collaborate varies, of course, from the implicit to the explicit, and from the token to the literal; the guiding characteristic is that the stage uses some form of the "you" address in its relation to the audience. One could think of this as a "we" voice in the sense that the audience joins the actors in the stage enterprise, but I prefer to retain the strict sense of "you" as the *spoken to* in the act of speech. In short, if "we" speaks to itself, it subdivides into "I" and "you." In general, this mode may be symbolized by the comic aside which presumes that the audience is in complicity with the setting of traps and deceits—or, to put it another way, the actor plays a character who lives in a world that includes the audience. For the most part, this is only a fictional assumption the play now and then indulges through certain characters (typically the clever servant), since it would be difficult for comedy to get anything done if it had to include the audience in all the developments. Besides, the actor who plays *to* the audience in the aside or the monologue is usually well within the play world, since the audience he addresses is only the idea of an audience. The audience actually has the status of a confidant character in neo-classical tragedy, unlike the real audience that modern participation theater tries to involve quite literally in the play. But the comic aside, together with the conventional prologue and epilogue, suggests a generic liberty that most comedy takes with its audience. The current of this liberty is not simply reference to the audience, but the comic project itself: the production of laughter.

A useful way to discuss the collaborative mode of performance is to contrast the relation of comedy and tragedy, as polar opposites, to their audiences. We often say that comedy arouses laughter and tragedy tears. The fact is, it is melodrama that arouses tears: tragedy arouses silence. The point of the distinction is that tragedy is a noncollaborative form, as usually performed. Tragedy creates an empathic experience wherein we are dissolved in what could be called a magnificent loneliness, felt most deeply in the absolute stillness of the auditorium when tragic characters say such things as "Thou shalt come no more." What the audience shares in such moments, and in the play at large, is less important than what isolates each spectator vicariously in the experience. Each spectator may be feeling roughly the same thing, and the actors may know that the whole house is, as Hamlet says, "wonder-wounded," but it is a private thing, as metaphysical experience usually is, and the tragic play makes no nonrepresentational provision for exploiting it. What tragedy tends to give us, at the end, is a surrogate audience of survivors on stage who act out the emotion occurring in the auditorium.

A line like Kent's "Break, heart; I prithee, break!" serves as a lightning rod that grounds our own emotional investment in the play. In fact, we might pause here to notice that beneath Kent's line—and Kent's character in general—is a subtle collaborative tendency whereby serious drama manages to include its audience in the play without violating the representational convention. We might state it in the form of a proposition: There seems to be a need in drama, or in certain kinds of drama, for a character who, among his other duties, will serve as a delegate or extension of the audience itself—the audience forming a sort of constituency that demands representation on the stage. The Greek chorus, that so-called "ideal spectator," comes immediately to mind; but the chorus is not really a character, in my sense of the word, as much as a communal abstraction which tends, in its powerless ubiquity, to become an audience in its own right. One of the reasons, I suspect, that the chorus is so uninteresting to us today is that it makes such a spectacle of itself—it tends, in short, to have our emotions for us. This is not categorically a bad thing. For example, imagine what would happen if you were to think away the chorus of saddened survivors at the end of a Shakespeare tragedy (the most cathartic point of our involvement) and allow the hero to die alone and unattended, like a great tree falling in an empty forest. Obviously we would be missing that indispensable frame of social response from which the new and presumably wiser order will arise. But we would also be losing a dramatic representation of our own emotional investment in the play. Which is to say that we want the play to contain an audience to its own act.

I don't know how far to press this idea beyond Shakespeare and his contemporaries, in whose work it is particularly strong, except to say that it becomes less evident, or at least changes its character, as the heroic principle declines and the play's society becomes more uniform. In the modern era, for example, the real drama is the gradual isolation of the protagonist from any social context whatsoever. Society is quite often absent (as in Beckett), or when it isn't, it goes about its business or looks the other way (as in Chekhov). The emotion *we* have, consequently, is of a very different order and scarcely a cathartic one. Consider the final scene of *Hedda Gabler,* which is designed precisely to create the sense of an ironic gap between Hedda's private motives for taking her life and the ignorance of those who survive her. In short, put "Good god, people don't do such things!" against "Now cracks a noble heart" and you see how drastically our representation on the stage has fallen off over the years.

Obviously it is wrong to say that tragedy does not openly acknowledge its audience. In its evolution out of the morality play, Elizabethan tragedy never gave up its theatrical self-awareness. Characters like Aaron, Edmund, and Iago talk easily to the pit, or at least to the convention of the pit. But it is notable that they are all villains and planners of deceit and that they have much in common with the clown in the tragic subplot. In fact, the only characters in tragedy who work with the audience are clowns and villains. This practice, moreover, is not restricted to Elizabethan drama. Humor and treachery seem to gravitate naturally toward the footlights—humor because it is incomplete without the audience, and treachery because it is not necessary to waste good play time motivating it if the playwright can have the audience's blessing. The Elizabethan villain, like his descendant the nineteenth-century landlord villain, is what Kenneth Burke calls the playwright's playwright. He seems to say to us, "Pretend I'm just plain evil. If I am not interesting myself, I will be the cause of your interest in the others." Apart from Shakespeare's master-villains, who could hardly be called uninteresting, it is hard to feel anything for characters who are on such easy terms with us because they don't seem to be undergoing anything but a play. They exist, one might say, in a limbo on the audience side of tragic seriousness. It would be unthinkable for a character like Lear or Macbeth—or even Hamlet, who is brother to the clown—to peer familiarly into the pit, because there is something in the abridgment of aesthetic distance that gives the lie to tragic character and pathos. A character who addresses the audience immediately takes on some of the audience's objectivity and superiority to the play's world. This is true even of modern narrator-protagonists like Arthur Miller's Quentin and Tennessee Williams's Tom Wingfield. They have survived tragedy, like Horatio, and, as the line goes in *Lear*, it is not the worst as long as you are alive to say it was the worst.

In cathartic terms, laughter is the dialectical opposite of tragic silence. As everyone knows, it is hard to laugh in a half-empty theater and it is even harder to act the comedy that is supposed to release the laughter. In one of his Letters to B, Kierkegaard asks his friend, "Answer me honestly . . . : do you ever really laugh when you are alone?" He concludes that you have to be "a little more than queer" if you do.[8] It follows that the genre that produces laughter for its living is the most social of all the dramatic forms, except possibly the masque, just as tragedy is the most nonsocial, at least from the standpoint of emotional logic. Tragedy, the early Lukács says, is "a science of death-moments, of conscious last moments when the soul has already given up the broad richness of existence and clings only to what it most deeply and intimately owns."[9] Comedy, one might add, is a science of life-moments, of an assurance that "the broad richness of existence" is all that really matters and that death can always be deferred. I am not assigning the performance of all comedy to the collaborative mode but only suggesting that comedy, as an extension of its theme, encourages the rapprochement of art and reality in a way that tragedy, as an extension of its theme, does not.

The social principle of comedy does not stop with comedy proper: comedy's next-door neighbors are realism and irony, and what energizes both realism and irony is the critique of social life that rests at the base of comedy. For example, I originally thought of the Brechtian actor as performing primarily in the self-expressive mode because he was, to a noticeable degree, *still* a performer standing just outside of his role. But this isn't really self-expressiveness in the sense that the performance, the virtuosity, is the center of attention; this detachment, or coming forth, of the

8. Søren Kierkegaard, *Either/Or,* trans. Walter Lowrie (Garden City, N.Y.: Doubleday & Co., 1959), 2: 331–32.
9. Georg Lukács, *Soul and Form,* trans. Anna Bostock (Cambridge: MIT Press, 1974), p. 161.

Brecht actor is a strategy for keeping the spectator on the objective wavelength in his hearing of the play. Moreover, the Brecht actor, as Paul Hernadi writes, "must no doubt identify with the author or the director at least as much as he identifies with 'himself', the psychophysical substratum of the character he is playing."[10] In other words, if he remains a performer, he is a company performer. Obviously, the Brecht actor can find all sorts of self-expressive fissures in the Brecht text, but as an actor who has a distinctly non-representational relation to the audience, he works primarily in the collaborative mode.

By an obvious association, we might draw an analogy between the second-personal voice and the epic, which we would oppose to the first-personal (or self-expressive) lyric. Perhaps Frye's term *epos,* or a work of oral address, is more appropriate. But I am thinking of epic as the form in which the poet speaks to his countrymen about national matters. He usually uses the third-personal, or narrative, point of view ("Then Hector rose up and slew them all"), but implicit in the manner of the exchange is the familiarity and sacredness of the matter. The epic addresses an audience of the initiated, for there would be little point in an epic poet singing about the heroic feats of another nation. As a form we have adapted to the theater, we would probably have to assign most epic acting (of, say, Shakespeare's Roses octology) to the third, or representational mode, along with tragedy. But Brecht's actor is

10. Paul Hernadi, "The Actor's Face as the Author's Mask: On the Paradox of Brechtian Acting," *Yearbook of Comparative Criticism* 7 (1976): 133.

peculiar in that he wants to speak to his countrymen about national matters they should hear about but, for the most part, not emulate. In other words, he wants to expel something from national character. So he speaks to them, as we have said, schizophrenically, with a self-criticism about what he is doing as a character. Hence he aligns the audience empathically with his critical self, not the self he is portraying. It is a strategy similar to that of the preacher who says, "I stand before you a sinner," the confession itself serving to alienate him from his sin. As Brecht uses it, this strategy is substantively ironic: it is a way of denouncing your sin in the act of performing it. But comedy is never far off in Brecht's world.

Is it possible to have theater by speaking directly to the audience, bypassing the entire pretense of representation and self-expression? This is the assumption of Peter Handke's *Offending the Audience.* Ostensibly, this "play" denies that it belongs to any category of theater performance. The four "speakers" are not actors; they act nothing, they do not speak to each other, and they do not speak for themselves, as characters ("Our speaking is our acting"). There is no plot, no scenery ("These boards don't signify a world. They are part of the world"). There is no lighting arrangement that isolates the speakers from the audience. Everything that typifies and nourishes theater has been eliminated except the structure of the actor /audience relationship, and the content of the play is devoted to reversing even this vestige of theater. In effect, the purpose of the play is not to offend the audience but to make the audience the hero, the event, the topic.

Can this be called a play? The answer is: Of course. The actors have not departed the stage to be replaced by "speakers." The actors are simply representing speakers who are denying they are actors. And there is scenery in the conspicuous absence of scenery. And there is lighting that is perfectly adequate to the purpose of shedding light on the master peripety of the play: the audience's recognition that it has, in old-fashioned tragicomic terms, had the tables turned on it. In short, there is pretense all over the piece. If a Handke actor were to forget his lines he would be in the same pickle as the Brechtian or any other actor. And Handke is wonderfully aware of all this. In fact, one of his speakers says, "This piece is classical," without spelling out just how classical it is.

The originality of the play lies in what we might call its "you-ness," or the particular level on which the rapprochement of audience and theater is effected. I doubt very much whether Rousseau would have appreciated Handke's project, but there is a passage in Derrida's essay on Rousseau that is as descriptive of what *Offending the Audience* is up to as it is of Rousseau's longing for a spectacle of "presence":

But what is a stage which presents nothing to the sight? It is the place where the spectator, presenting himself as spectacle, will no longer be either seer [*voyant*] or voyeur, will efface within himself the difference between the actor and the spectator, the represented and the representer, the object seen and the seeing object. With that difference, an entire series of oppositions will deconstitute themselves one by one. Presence will be full, not as an object which is *present* to be seen, to give itself to intuition as an empirical unit or as an *eidos* holding itself *in front of* or *up against*; it will be full as the intimacy of a self-presence, as the consciousness or the sentiment of self-proximity, of self-sameness [*propriété*].[11]

And, in fact, the you-ness turns out to be a kind of me-ness. The strange thing is that the speakers do not become intimate with the audience in *manner* but in *matter*. They always treat the audience as an assembled group, but they increasingly refer to those aspects of individual privacy—blinking, breathing, swallowing, sitting, smelling, sweating—that are irresistible attention-getters because speech has become a kind of anatomical probe ("Why, how terribly self-conscious you are"). In other words, if someone says to you, "You've got food on your chin," the body instantly drops whatever else it is doing and deals with that problem. This is the most offensive part of the show, but as the speakers say, being offensive in any context is a good way to "tear down a wall."

The whole process of the play is a disgorging of theater into the world. The play is a prologue, it tells us, to the rest of the audience's life:

It is not the prologue to another piece but the prologue to what you did, what you are doing, and what you will do. You are the topic. This piece is the prologue to the topic. It is the prologue to your practices and customs. It is the prologue to your actions. It is the prologue to your inactivity. It is the prologue to your lying down, to your sitting, to your standing, to your walking. It is the prologue to the plays and to the seriousness of your life. It is also the prologue to your future visits to the theater. It is also the prologue to all other prologues. This piece is world theatre.[12]

11. Derrida, *Of Grammatology*, p. 306.
12. Handke, *Kaspar and Other Plays*, p. 28.

The logic here is much like that of Brecht's theater of alienation: to send the audience back to the world with a new awareness. But there is nothing political about Handke's program. What his play has attempted to do, as prologue, is to transfer the audience's normal attentiveness to the theater event back upon itself, back into the world of pre- and post-theatrical life. It is not a program that is likely to work beyond the trip home, any more than Brecht's or any other socially revisionary program. But that is not what concerns us here. *Offending the Audience* carries the collaborative principle to an intricate extreme and is an excellent tool for opening up the nature of the theater process and experience to students who haven't thought much about the phenomenal relation of theater to living, or of play to audience. For Handke's play defines theater as it dismantles it and creates theater as it claims to devastate its premises. As Douglas Hofstadter might say, there is a "strange loopiness" about it. That is, as the speakers strip away one level of theater after another, leaving the audience in this state of self-enlightenment, "we unexpectedly find ourselves right back where we started"[13]—in the theater. Handke, like Gödel in mathematics, is using theater self-referentially, as an explanation of what it is and how it works. I suspect that with the right performers—and certainly the right audience—it might do to one's emotions what the Epimenidean paradox ("This sentence is false") does to the head.

13. Hofstadter, *Gödel, Escher, Bach,* p. 10.

The general idea of the representational mode is implicit in much of what we have said about the others. In effect, the self-expressive and the collaborative modes of performance display theater in its extraverted personality, or what we might call its courtship plumage. In one case, the performer comes forth and astonishes us with the possibilities of virtuosity; in the other, theater says to the spectator, "Why should we pretend that all this is an illusion. We are in this together." Perhaps the more persistent source of theater's seductive power is the drama of its subject, or, to use Aristotle's term in a very loose sense, its *praxis.* Theater's endless mission is to be *about* something, not about men but about their actions, wherein they are happy or unhappy. Theater is, after all, representation, and all that I have said here by way of adjusting our perspective on the mimetic principle does not reduce its importance, even in the case of opera or the mime. One could argue that dance, in some of its modern forms, does not require a subject to be imitated: for example, a dance called "Variations on Sphericality." But the success of one's argument would depend on how well one could prove that sphericality itself, as a pattern of organization the body submits itself to, wasn't a subject of representation.

Behind the representational mode of performance, and our perception of it, is the shared sense that we come to the theater primarily to see a play, not a performance. Continuing my analogy of the self-expressive with the lyric and the collaborative with the epic, we might describe the representational as the *dramatic* key of theatrical presentation—the key of *he, she, it,* and *they*—in which we look in objectively on a drama with a beginning, middle, and end that is occurring before our eyes. All of the actor's artistic energies now seem to be bent toward becoming his character and, for the audience, they cease to be artistic energies and become the facts of his character's nature. It has nothing to do with credulity; the audience simply sees through the sign language of the art to the signified beyond. The play is not a text, classic or brand-new, out of which theater magic can be made; it is now an enactment of significant human experience. Even if the play is the most trivial comedy, it is something we can disappear into because it is *about* people (who are, now and then, both trivial and funny). So the virtuosity now lies in the power of the subject, the collaboration in the mutual agreement by actor and audience on the value and appropriateness of the subject to the community of men. At the beginning of the Olivier *Hamlet* film, we are told by Olivier's disembodied voice that this is the story of a man who could not make up his mind. Plays do not normally do this sort of self-foretelling, except in prologues, but implicitly there is always the voice of our understanding telling us that what we will see in this window / mirror is a replica of our own "coulds" and "could nots." Olivier's voice-over, like the dimming of the houselights in the theater, is a bridge by which we leave the world and enter it at another time and place.

Before moving to the representational mode, I should emphasize that my treatment of these three modes as if they occurred *purely* is strictly a convenience of definition. It is precisely our ability to integrate them or to arrest one or another of them in our perceptual attention that lends the unique depth and texture to the theater experience. Theater is not simply an interesting fiction being performed, it is a *collaboration,* a set of mannerly assumptions about our participation in these other two modes of perception (this is why a rehearsal is not a performance). So there is no incompatibility among the modes: they coexist continuously (at some level) on the same stage; one may hear them together or in succession, somewhat as one may choose to hear the oboe or the violin or the full orchestra.

Perhaps some elaboration of the point is in order. Suppose a character speaks directly, collaboratively, to the audience (without, of course, stepping out of character): Is the representational aspect of the moment diminished? Perhaps, but not necessarily. It is really a question of the kind of representation that has been established by the play (or by the production). One of the assumptions of straight realism, for example, is that there is no acknowledgment of the audience's presence because the play is dead serious about being real, and it would hardly have served the interests of a play like *Awake and Sing* if Morris Carnovsky had played some of his lines to an audience that was not supposed to be there. But a violation of this principle, properly prepared, is not incompatible with all forms of realism, as we see in Tom Wingfield's "This play is memory" speech at the beginning of *The Glass Menagerie.* The purpose of the collaborative principle here, of course, was to embed the drama in the wider frame of Tom's reflective consciousness, no less realistic for being outside or beyond the action. In other words, when the collaborative mode is invoked for thematic purposes, it is no more destructive to the stage illusion, even a highly realistic one, than iambic pentameter or song in opera. It is simply a means of adjusting the audience's *illusionary* nearness to the action.

As a way of widening the idea, let us look briefly at a

symptomatic example from the theater of Shakespeare. When Edmund collaboratively lets us in on his play to undo his brother, we are still well within the illusionary world of *King Lear* which includes (for certain characters at least) access to an imaginary listener. We are, in fact, only one short step beyond soliloquy, in which the character tends to speak as much about himself as to himself. Hence the illusionary realness of Shakespeare's theater, which offers actors such wonderful opportunities to "show themselves off," always contains a subtle collaborative element, or at least an option to address the audience. I suspect that the function of this option was not simply to allow the play to acknowledge its own fictionality, but to keep one theatrical eye on the very palpable crowd ringing the stage. It is well to remember that realism, as we know it, is substantially a product of the indoor evening theater, the ideal stage for treating the audience as an unsuspected voyeur rather than as an invited guest. But Shakespeare's stage had a built-in PR problem in the sense that its audience, drawn from a relatively wide social base, was very visible, very near (if not on) the stage, and probably very vocal. Part of it loved Termagant and Herod, and part of it must have loved Viola and Cordelia. I'm not suggesting there was a discipline problem, only a diplomatic one—in fact, one of the oldest problems in communication: how to suit the manner of speaking to the manner in which the listener listens. For such a case, the rule of thumb might be: the more sociable the audience the more sociability must somehow be built into the act. No doubt this whole speaking relationship came about naturally and unproblematically (and could be attributed to many other influences); I am simply trying to illustrate how the collaborative element may be said to adjust the play to its social scene.

Given the emphasis on the subject matter in the representational mode, our problem becomes one of leaving the actor per se and looking more closely at how subjects get into the theater and how they behave once they are there. Before doing so, however, it must be stressed that the representational mode of performance does not imply a realistic style of acting, singing, dancing, or production. Or, to put it more accurately, what we call realism is no closer to reality than many forms of representation we would call stylized. It is hard to believe the anonymous biographer of Aeschylus when he says that the chorus of *The Eumenides* "so terrified the crowd that children died and women suffered miscarriage."[14] What we do learn from the reference, however, is the basic fact beneath all representation: the suspension of disbelief does not depend in the least on what we would today call a photographic likeness of the image to reality. It depends only on the power of the image to serve as a channel for what of reality is of immediate interest to the audience. In effect, this brings us to the study of conventions that we touched upon in the opening chapter. This is a topic that might occupy an entire book. Here I want only to illustrate briefly how *the subject* of the representation comes forth and commands our interest. The fact is, most theater, in Roland Barthes's term, "prattles"; that is, it drifts on the current of fashion, content with predigested food, with "what the public wants." This is not in any sense

14. A. M. Nagler, *Sources of Theatrical History* (New York: Theatre Annual, 1952), p. 5.

an indictment of theater (the same could be said of any art), but an acknowledgment of one of its several responsibilities. But it is self-evident that any image—even a prattling one—has a life cycle we might characterize as a movement from innovation to convention to cliché, often with a final stage of self-parody. The new image explodes with life and ends up struggling for life, wearing out. Again, the simple fate of all art images is the curse of familiarity. "After we see an object several times," Shklovsky says, "we begin to recognize it. The object is in front of us and we know about it, but we do not see it."[15] Thus all images gravitate toward invisibility. To become accustomed to something means that one no longer sees it as self-given. As Brecht said of his watch: When it has told you the time, it has nothing more to say to you.[16]

The innovative stage of an image is characterized by enthusiastic overstatement. The new image, like new fashions, goes too far. This is not a fault but a characteristic of enthusiasm and discovery, though technically it is observable as such only retrospectively, from the standpoint of later refinement. For example, in O'Neill's early plays the discovery of psychology led to what we now perceive as embarrassing excesses in unrealistic devices (the long asides of *Strange Interlude,* overexplicit self-psychoanalysis) or to over-realism (the use of regional dialect and street slang, long drunk scenes). Many of these same enthusiasms had long been refined out of continental realism, but images tend to be reborn *ad ovum* for new audiences. To take another image, virtually at its source, one can imagine how in

15. Shklovsky, "Art as Technique," p. 13.
16. Brecht, *Brecht on Theatre,* p. 144.

the early 1890s London audiences who had just seen Ibsen's daring *Hedda Gabler* or *A Doll's House,* or had read Hardy's scandalous *Tess of the d'Urbervilles,* would have reacted to a big scene like Paula Tanqueray's exit from Pinero's play. What probably interested the audience most is her closing speech, and unfortunately it is too long to quote. But it may be summarized as a young wife's prophetic vision of the day when age will have taken her beauty and she will be seen by her husband "under a queer, fantastic light at night or in the glare of the morning." This is the last we hear from her, for, like Hedda and so many of her sisters in misery, she rushes off to her suicide. If the speech doesn't provide a motive (she has more immediate ones), it dramatizes graphically the "physical revulsion" that might make suicide a reasonable option. For flavor, here is a sample of what is in store for her in a few short years:

A worn-out creature—broken up, very likely, some time before I ought to be—my hair bright, my eyes dull, my body too thin or too stout, my cheeks raddled and ruddled—a ghost, a wreck, a caricature, a candle that gutters, call such an end what you like![17]

She may even, she says earlier, "drift the way of the others" and resort to cosmetics "and those messes." This speech is probably a good example of what Shaw meant by the word "Pinerotic" insofar as it seems to be more interested in caressing its subject than in getting Mrs. Tanqueray into a suicidal mood. Hearing the

17. Arthur Wing Pinero, *The Second Mrs. Tanqueray* (Boston: Walter N. Baker, 1894), p. 170.

speech today, an audience familiar, for example, with Blanche DuBois's violent fear of the light bulb, would certainly be amused that a character so beside herself with anxiety would become such an eloquent raconteur of her own decay. But the image value of the speech in 1893 lies in the fact that it sounded a more or less un-spoken concern that had not yet had its moment on the London stage. The lot of the ostracized woman had been a theme of realism since Dumas *fils* and Hebbel, but it was not until Ibsen and the new "sexual" novel that it took on such private psychological complexion; and the important thing was to hold it up to the strong candlelight of the stage and turn it, ever so slowly (like those slow-motion blood baths in Sam Peckinpah's early films) until its anatomy was fully displayed. The common principle of innovative imagery from Seneca's journey through Hell to realism's journey into the causal past to Absurdity's absurdities seems to be that if something is good, more of it is better. Little is left to the imagination because the eye and the ear have not yet had their fill.

The innovative obviously gives way quickly to the conventional phase of the image. Conventions, Harry Levin has said, "are seldom recognized until they have been nearly outgrown."[18] Another way to say this is that function disguises form: when content is interest-ing you are not apt to notice the container (for example, only when an actor becomes boring do you notice that he has habits). The conventional phase of an image is what we might term the semiotically strong phase.

18. Harry Levin, "Notes on Convention," in *Perspectives of Criti-cism* (Cambridge: Harvard University Press, 1950), p. 66.

What I mean by this is expressed in a passage from Bergson's *Matter and Memory* which is, in effect, a phenomenological statement antedating the passage I quoted from Shklovsky:

In fact, there is no perception which is not full of memories. With the immediate and present data of our senses we mingle a thousand details out of our past experience. In most cases these memories supplant our actual perceptions, of which we then recall only a few hints, thus using them merely as "signs" that recall to us former images. The convenience and the rapidity of perception are bought at this price.[19]

Bergson is not referring specially to art images here but to any form of matter that is *perceived* and thus falls midway between thing and sign. But the statement would certainly apply to the art image. In any case, by semiotically strong I am referring to this inrush of memory on perception that allows the new image to begin its work of linking the stage to the world of meaning outside. As an image becomes phenomenally weaker it becomes (for a time) significatively stronger—which is to say that it no longer stands in its own way.

The semiotically vital stage of an image is marked by a drive that might be characterized in two ways. On the one hand, the image strives to become more efficient or streamlined: this is one way in which it guards itself against the audience's growing familiarity. An image's relation to its audience, if we can speak in such terms, is

19. Henri Bergson, *Matter and Memory,* trans. Nancy Margaret Paul and W. Scott Palmer (London: G. Allen & Co.), p. 24.

like the conversation of married people: it needs to say less and less in order to communicate. But on the other hand, it faces the task of escaping its own streamlined stereotype. Hence its migration to new contents. This is the stage in which it names all of the social variations it can express: first adultery in the city, then adultery on the farm, then aboard ship, and so on. Once the theater is armed with a paradigm it will not be satisfied until it has tried out every available content. Ideally, the progress will be from surprise to surprise; that is, the next variation should contain an unexpected numerator that will display the denominator (adultery) in fresh accents. A convenient model of both processes might be the popular joke: "How many X's does it take to change a light bulb?" We all know this joke began as a variation of the so-called Polish joke; but it proved an extremely efficient device for satirizing anything in the culture that accumulates a reputation for stubbornness or "doing its own thing." Because culture constantly replenishes the joke's form with new contents, it will probably have a long life as a graphic condensation of our addictions.

There is no way to be more specific about the evolution of the image because images vary in their resistance or submissiveness to conventionalization (an animal, as I've suggested, is a resistant image, a chair a submissive one), in their potential for combination and permutation, and in their durability. It is only a matter of the time it takes an image to fill up with emptiness. An image might have its season in the sun and die of old age (Cushman and Bernhardt playing Hamlet), only to be resurrected in another age (Anderson playing Hamlet). Or it may achieve immortality, or such immortality as history permits. For example, in 1830 the actor playing Hugo's Hernani stood downstage with his back to the audience through most of the opening act. It does not matter whether this was the first instance of "the theater of the back," though it does matter that the scene is France. (In England it would have been less memorable because, as Voltaire said, "An Englishman says what he will, a Frenchman what he can.") In one gesture this production of *Hernani* articulated the root principle of naturalism long before its time. Implicit in "the back" is the whole concept of the fourth wall and its presumption that the stage is a replica of the real world and not a palace of virtuosity from which the real world is kept at bay by firm rules—among them the rule that the actor played *to* his audience at all times. The back, however, was apparently slow to catch on and only began to flourish in the later century with the naturalists and Antoine. It needed, in other words, the kind of play that would justify it. In fact, by 1910—if we can believe Frank Wedekind—it had passed prematurely from the status of a convention to that of an annoyance: "The works of the naturalistic playwrights owed their uncommonly rapid dissemination not least of all to the advantage that they were childishly simple to act. . . . The actor stuck his hands in his pocket, placed himself with his back to the audience next to the prompt-box, and waited with the greatest of ease until he heard the word called out to him."[20] To the extent that this complaint was widespread it was undoubtedly the result of overuse (like swearing in the plays of the

20. Frank Wedekind, "The Art of Acting: A Glossary," in *Masterpieces of Modern German Theatre*, ed. Robert W. Corrigan (New York: Macmillan, 1975), pp. 224–25.

1960s), but the back obviously survived because it was not so much an image as *a way of being* on the stage. Today, we no longer perceive it as a convention but as normal stage posture. It is natural, not naturalistic. Today's naturalistic parallel might be frontal nudity—which began, we might recall, as a "back" view—now well on its way into the conventional stage and, barring a moral revolution, destined for permanent service.

It would perhaps be more convenient to talk in broad terms of image systems, or subjects, rather than in terms of individual images, since all images in the theater occur in an "informational polyphony,"[21] or a dense context in which they interact and give life to each other. As a typical model we might take the evolution of villainy in English drama of the Shakespeare period. Everyone will recognize the phrase "Be ruled by me," which occurs regularly, especially in those scenes in which villains are meeting "in hugger-mugger" and one of them must be persuaded to dirty business by the other. But one notices that the reasons *why* someone should be ruled by someone else become more telegraphic as we progress through the period. That is, the phrase becomes a substitute, or shorthand, for any or all of the standard motives the audience knows from past plays (in somewhat the same way that the sign *Keep off the grass* is shorthand for a set of known motives pertaining to the sociology of landscaping). But this short-cutting in the display of persuasion is only a symptom of a gradual shift in the sensational emphasis of onstage violence itself. If I may amend a proposition from Kenneth Burke: The growing fascination with the forms of

21. Barthes, *Critical Essays,* pp. 261–62.

violence leads to a corresponding atrophy in the motivational psychology behind violence.[22] On the whole, Elizabethan drama was very casual about motivating anything, but the spectacle of arousing and plotting revenge (or motivation) is much more central in early drama. For example, Hieronimo is plunged into grief by the murder of his son, is driven mad by grief, and kills sensationally in his madness late in the play. And so with Hamlet. Whereas, in later plays (for example Webster) motives are murky and it is usually sufficient to hate someone to have him dispatched. In sum, long simmering revenges like Hamlet's or Othello's fell out of fashion, and attention shifted to the interesting things one could do to victims once revenge was set in motion. Now Elizabethan drama, from start to finish, is probably the bloodiest in theater history. It is hard to top early plays like *The Jew of Malta, The Tragedy of Hoffman, Selimus,* and *Titus Andronicus* for pure gore; but these plays are naive when compared to some of the death scenes in Tourneur, Webster, and Massinger. Here the theatrical shock falls not only on the number of deaths or their brutality, but on the ingenuity of the murderers whose devices remind you of Rube Goldberg machines in their intricacy. In fact, some characters seem to have been admitted to the play only for the spectacle of their departure through someone's "witty cruelty," as one of Massinger's characters puts it. Massinger's best contribution to this spectacle is a play in

22. Kenneth Burke, *Counter-Statement* (Los Altos, Calif.: Hermes Publication, 1953), p. 33. Burke's statement reads: "The hypertrophy of the psychology of information is accompanied by the corresponding atrophy of the psychology of form."

which a Roman actor (who has been doomed by Caesar) is mercifully allowed to die "on the job" while acting out a death scene with Caesar.

We see much the same pattern of evolution in the
modern drama of indoor menace from Strindberg to
Pinter. Strindberg's characters, at the dawn of the new
psychology, are very "forthcoming," to use a Pinter
word; they tell us what is on their minds, and of course
it must have been shocking to hear wives being as
openly nefarious as Laura is to the Captain in *The Father.* But by the time we get to Pinter all this is old psychology—perhaps not the psychology itself as much as
the drama of its revelation—and we are left with the
bare fact of menace into which one can read all sorts of
Freudian and post-Freudian motives. To look at still
another evolution: Chekhov's plays (among others)
would have been impossible in the early stages of realism devoted to exploring the social and psychological
causes of the protagonist's inevitable isolation. (A good
example might be the scene in *La Dame aux Camélias* in
which M. Duval isolates Marguerite Gautier from his
son in a long explanation of why society cannot accom-
modate their love to its "exacting standards.") Chekhov's drama assumes all of this as a part of the foundation
of its realism, and concentrates on the various private
strategies for dealing, or not dealing, with isolation.
Chekhov probably didn't think about this, any more
than Pinter thought of Strindberg and Ibsen. It was simply the state of the art. It was, as Eliot would say, part
of his inheritance, part of "the mind of Europe" that
forgets or abandons nothing en route. The subtext of
Chekhov, in other words, is the unforgotten text of the
early realists.

The cliché stage of the image speaks for itself. The vein has, temporarily at least, run dry. The spectator not only sees through the signifier but through the signified as well. For example, the benevolent characters of eighteenth-century sentimental drama eventually cease to remind one of benevolence or anything else; they are simply ciphers in a boring formula that no longer accounts for life satisfactorily. Hence Goldsmith's cry—*enough* of the virtues and distresses of private life! The more interesting stage is that of self-parody where the drama pokes fun at its own ossifications. Let us imagine a moment in history in which by some Borgesian fluke the theater became enamored with plays with ticking clocks, running fountains, and child actors with pet dogs. This was, so to speak, the winning combination, and no play was really safe unless it contained at least one or two of these attractions. But in time this winning combination becomes a standard formula and things reach a crisis. Audiences begin seeing through everything: they see only the signs of a weary stage. The crisis might temporarily arrest itself in self-parody, which injects into the formula the in-joke of its own immanent suicide. This is a highly collaborative moment in which stage and audience share an understanding about plays as plays. It is probably very brief, and the *coup de grace* may occur (homage to Chekhov) when an adult character in a new and innovative play enters and says to another adult character, "Let's sit down here and talk. Thank god there are no dogs or children about." And the audience cheers. This seems farfetched until one remembers that this is how Euripides put the finishing touches on poor Aeschylus in the recognition scene of his *Electra* and, more generally, resolved the "matter of Troy" itself in plays like *Helen* and *Orestes.*

To sum up: we should think of these pronominal modes as points of reference rather than as discrete phases in our perception of the actor. In other words, having separated them out we should probably allow them to fall back together into a perceptual synthesis, bearing in mind that even when they upstage each other they are as much cooperating as competing. The advantage of thinking about the actor in such terms is not that we learn anything new about him, but that we have a better basis for seeing how his performance awakens our interest, not only as individuals sitting at a play but as members of a social species that commissions the actor to enact plays about our various concerns and addictions. There is probably no such thing as a period in which one mode dominates the others, though certainly in the era of the star system the actor's virtuosity—or at least his reputation for virtuosity—drew the audience to the theater more so than the subject of the play. And in the 1960s something in our culture gave rise to a rash of collaborative plays, or what we might call a return to Rousseau naturalism in which the actor strived, with our consent, to make theater once again an enterprise that included the audience. Finally, we might point to moments in theater history when the play itself became the instrument through which we examined emerging veins of social behavior or revived old veins: the new social drama of the late nineteenth century, the American Agit-prop theater, the various revivals of romantic and poetic drama, realistic plays about drug addiction, homosexuality, deranged children, and so on. But even such emphatic moments do not circumscribe theater's various appeals at any particular time. And so it is with the appeal of the actor, who is probably as complex a phenomenon as the theater he serves. The problem with the actor, in fact, is that he is *there,* before us, *all at once,* in one sense the primary medium of theater, in another its end and purpose. My intention here is not to offer a complete phenomenology of his art but to treat it as an act of speech, a discourse, one might say, on *our* behavior, that can be broken down into the pronominal triad that is the basis of all speech. The actor acts out our ways of referring to the things of the world. Or, translated into the terms of our perception of his art: he does this by becoming in part a thing himself, in part by doing a thing, and in part by sharing it. Perhaps the best way to recover a sense of the complexity of the performer / spectator relationship is to concentrate a great deal of attention on what seems to be its definitive collaborative moment— the moment in which the actor, any actor in history, stands before the audience at the end of the play, unencumbered by the illusion or by his art, and bows to its applause. The phenomenological question would be: What is this friendly conversation between bow and applause all about? How does this ending contain and sum up the "ends" of playing, as I have been discussing them here?

The curtain call belongs most broadly to the tradition of the parting, the introduction of the speaker, the invocation, and the recessional—in other words, to the whole realm of formal beginnings and endings whereby we punctuate the events of social life and rescue them from the indifferent drift of time. Consider how intolerable it would be if at the end of a performance of *Hamlet* the actors simply rose from the dead, brushed themselves off, and retired to their dressing rooms like workers punching out at quitting time.

To be more specific, the curtain call is a seam in social nature: actually, a beginning *and* an ending, a return and a farewell. Kierkegaard might have assigned it to the "category of the interesting" insofar as it is a turning point or "border category" between aesthetics and manners.[23] In any case, since a seam by definition contains only what it joins, to talk about the curtain call at all is to talk about both art and manners, in this instance two forms of roleplaying. In Aristotelian terms, we could describe it as the reversal and recognition of the actor/audience relationship: both have been liberated from the strain of art; they have come out of hiding, out of the slumber of the illusion, as Puck says in the epilogue of *Midsummer Night's Dream,* and have become "friends."

As a more useful metaphor we might think of the curtain call as a decompression chamber halfway between the depths of art and the thin air of reality. For obvious reasons, the actors remain in costume but not in character. Or, not exactly in character; for it often happens that an actor, if not the entire cast, will deliber-

23. Søren Kierkegaard, *Fear and Trembling and The Sickness Unto Death,* trans. Walter Lowrie (New York: Anchor Books, 1954), p. 92.

ately retain traces of his role, as in the continuance of mannerisms, or *lazzi*, for comic effect (comedians, as we say, are "always on stage"); or, in heavier plays, a general gravity of mood in which, say, the actor who played Hamlet remains vaguely Hamletic beneath a "house" smile. But this is taken by both audience and cast as evidence of the fanciful power of the play to out- last itself. As Bergson would say, it has encrusted its spirit on the actors who have just performed it. And on the audience as well. (To avoid a set of irrelevant prob- lems, I am assuming throughout a combination of ideal conditions: the perfect production, the most receptive audience, one of theater's most engrossing plays.)

There is also an unintentional, and far more inter- esting, sense in which the actor remains in character— or, to put it a better way, the character remains in the actor, like a ghost. It is not at all a clean metamorpho- sis. The audience does not forget Hamlet just because the actor who imitated him now takes a bow in his own right for having done so. What we see now is not the unvarnished actor, fresh from Hamlet, but the real side of the Hamlet phenomenon. Hamlet's character has simply been suppressed, as you might suppress a skill or a temper. Conceivably, Hamlet might pour forth from the tap, on cue. In fact, looking naively through a psychological crack in the theatrical sham, one might even suspect that the actor's performance was an open display of a hidden, or at least possible, self. Doesn't the playing of Hamlet, after all, require a dredging up of a Hamlet from somewhere within? Or, let us say that in giving this unique embodiment to the text the actor has now annexed Hamlet, like a colony, to himself. For it is part of the myth of the actor that each role is a kind of conquest, or permanent acquisition, that swells his holdings and leads eventually to a famous face. We do not think of an actor's portrayal of a role as being sealed off in the past tense, but as floating in a past absolute, as if it were, like the role itself, outside time. Not only is it preserved in the communal memory as part of the history of the play, leaving its imprint (for a time) on the text, but due to the repetitive element in all style, remnants keep popping up in the later work of the actor. For example, certain mannerisms of Olivier's Othello—the darting glance, the emphasis on certain kinds of values, the deft economy of gesture—remind one of the "younger" Hamlet. Of course, this is only Olivier repeating himself, but it is Hamlet who is fleetingly remembered. There is *still* a Hamlet in Olivier.

I am hardly suggesting that any of this passes through an audience's mind during the curtain call. These are simply attempts to ground our perception of lingering character in subliminal extremities. The mysterious bonding of actor and character always implies a slightly supernatural achievement. Who else but the actor is privileged to live life at such speed and intensity? Who else but the actor—the only honest hypocrite, as Hazlitt said—can become a great person by pretending to be one? Here, of course, we are back on the subject of the actor's fame. Because we know him only as a stylization, a portable aesthetic object, we imagine that his real life is qualitatively a continuation of his life on stage: he leads the plot of a life, free of tedium, all of the routine necessities—eating, sleeping, driving to work—are simply omitted, as in a play. Even his character we imagine as a vague concoction of roles.[24] In short, our fascination with the actor is something of a romantic crush that transcends sexual lines (though the best illustration of the idea is Othello's seduction of Desdemona through the witchcraft of a partly invented life). As a consequence, when we see a great actor on stage there is always a slight element of disbelief. We know that it is Olivier who is playing Hamlet, as advertised; but there is a considerable gap between the myth of Olivier and the real actor up there on the stage. There is no satisfactory way to account for why Olivier has left the important business of leading his ideal life to appear here, in the flesh, before this cross section of local theatergoers. Surely there are ideal audiences waiting elsewhere, outside time, in what we somewhat parochially call "the world beyond."[25] But for any theater audience—privileged, as the cinema audience is not, to see a live performance—

24. Then there is H. L. Mencken's less friendly version of this same phenomenon: "He becomes a grotesque boiling down of all the preposterous characters he has ever impersonated. Their characteristics are seen in his manner, in his reactions to stimuli, in his point of view. He becomes a walking artificiality, a strutting dummy, a thematic catalogue of imbecilities" (*Prejudices: Second Series* [New York: Alfred A. Knopf, 1920], pp. 208–209). I wish to thank my student, Bonnie Bricker, for calling this passage to my attention.

25. There is of course the other side of the coin: the real actor, in person, is always slightly disappointing. For example, Diderot on Mlle. Clairon: "And hence it is that the player in private and the player on the boards are two personages, so different that one can scarcely recognize the player in private. The first time I saw Mlle. Clairon in her own house I exclaimed, by a natural impulse, 'Ah, mademoiselle, I thought you were at least a head taller!'" (*The Paradox of Acting,* p. 23).

there is no moment in which the actor is more ambiguously real than when he emerges from the play and
bows to us at this unstable border between two contradictory realms. He is one of us, and yet as he stands "in
borrowed robes" he is full of the allure of fiction. Not
only has he played Hamlet, but he somehow contains
him—as a form or a discipline (his way of bowing, for
example).

But this is to look at what passes in the curtain call
through only one eye of our binocular vision. In the
straightforward emotional sense Hamlet has been irre-
trievably lost with his death on stage. His story was indeed a fiction, but one that has amazed the very faculty
of eyes and ears. The thing we call catharsis arises, in
part at least, from the fact that we can be carried so ut-
terly into this dream by the actor only to have it come
to nothing, to be purged, as the lights dim. And what
we mourn is the double death of Hamlet the imaginary
character and Hamlet as a possibility in real nature. It is
simply saddening to think that Hamlet was a vivid lie.
Here we are brought against two overlapping para-
doxes of the theater: that something so intensely real
could lack the fundamental quality of the real (endurance); and that something so absolute as the history of
Hamlet could be contained in a "local habitation"
(technically, a theater stage) as a kind of brief seizure in
the real. Hence the inevitable analogy of theater and
dream: the enacted play is, in Sartre's term, an induced
dream,[26] the communal version of the dream journey
to the other reality, that private exception to the rules of
the possible. The astonished question of the dreamer is:

26. Sartre, *The Psychology of Imagination,* p. 252.

How is it possible to have been so thoroughly within a world that was within my own head? The return from the play world is like the awakening from the dream: it is always an abrupt fall into the mundane, fraught with the nostalgia of exile from an impossible land. And in this respect the living actor is our cushion. He stands before us in the curtain call as a consolation, a transition and an easement; he is not only the carnal remnant of Hamlet, but Hamlet's biographer and rhapsode, one who has known Hamlet intimately in that other vanished world by way of being, somewhat literally, in his shoes. He becomes, so to speak, a *real* Horatio who has survived, at one further remove, to tell Hamlet's story. It is possible that he bows as much for Hamlet, imprisoned on the legendary side of time, as for himself.

Precisely at the outbreak of applause, the fiction of the play is replaced by the fiction of manners. For instance, it is assumed that the actor will be on good behavior—congenial, if not humble—during the call. For one thing, this is the only possible defense against the numerical superiority of the audience. In other words, the actor is, in a sense, pretending that he is himself. He is seeking our approval (so the convention goes), or at least he has consented to accept it, like those canny politicians in Shakespeare who contrive to be called back by the crowd to accept the laurel they have seemingly not sought. In any case, it is not the moment for the actor to play Coriolanus and refuse to display his "wounds": the paint, the perspiration, the breathlessness, all the traces of having been through the role—or the role, like a fever, having been through him. Even the trace of fatigue, seen through this appreciative geniality, is in order because it suggests that this was hard work, though the work consisted wholly in making it seem no work at all. It is even appropriate that the actor be mildly embarrassed as he "stoops to our clemency" (the more insistent the applause, the greater the embarrassment). He is (so the convention goes) out of his element: performing *Hamlet* was one thing, facing all these people another. This is the fiction of the modest actor, and the fact that the modesty may be sincere makes it no less a fiction during the curtain call; for the modesty in this case is grounded in the fact that modesty in real life is a prized virtue, nowhere 'more so than among the famous. Here we touch on a larger sociological truth. In the aura of this honest submission to convention there is a faint reminder that we like genius to exhibit some minor human weakness. Einstein was a mediocre violinist; had he had been a great violinist, as well as a great physicist, we would have found and cherished some other weakness (ideally, an occasional carelessness in lower mathematics, as Hemingway is rumored to have got poor grades in English composition). This has nothing to do with cutting genius down to size, but only with humanizing it—that is, adding to its perfection the virtue of having noticeably risen out of our world. How satisfying it is to read about actors who return periodically to their hometowns, work "behind the scenes" for public causes, or remain married to unknowns, often for life. So it is natural that there is nothing more warmly received during the curtain call than a spontaneous disclosure of the human: a minor confusion in places, an embarrassment over a misbehaving prop, a paternal display of affection by the star for a new actor who was "brilliant," *any* sign of real, nonconventional life. In an extreme case (a frequent practice in Soviet theater) the actors might even applaud the audience—which translates into the communism of mutual respect and teamwork: "Your goodness has made it possible for us to be good."

To turn to my final question: What is it in the play, or in play itself, that authorizes this posture of the bowing actor, the eternal logo of the theater? From a purely aesthetic perspective, we may say that the curtain call is the necessary self-disclosure of the illusion, comparable to the shedding of masks at a costume party. It is no contradiction of this principle to add that certain forms of theater dispense with the curtain call altogether. For example, the closer a play comes to the religious, the less appropriate the curtain call. A play intended to bind the group together ritually, or to honor a mystery, would only violate its premise by seeking the profanity of applause. As a rule of thumb: in any play in which virtuosity is upstaged by mission—as in committed political drama—the curtain call is likely to be omitted or reduced to a perfunctory bow. But in most theater, the curtain call is a functional part of the psychology of ending. Without it, or without something like it, there remains the unresolved chord of the play's aesthetic causality. It is not a matter of confirming that *Hamlet* has been played by actors but of treating the senses to the conclusion of a known process. Aesthetically, the true ending of theater is not the passing of the stage illusion into the *et cetera* of its own afterplot ("Go, bid the soldiers shoot." *Exeunt marching*), but the ending of play itself.[27] Hence the curtain call is a means of dramatizing the all-but-forgotten truth that art has only used

27. Terence Hawkes briefly treats the curtain call along these same lines in "Opening Closure," *Modern Drama* 24 (September 1981): 356.

nature, as a parasite uses a host. The portraits in the mirror have all been an excuse for a display of the mirror's remarkable powers. It is true that we knew this all along, but the presentational basis of theater rests upon a double pretense: the play pretends that we don't exist (the fourth-wall convention) and we pretend that the play does (the willing suspension of disbelief). So it is always a pleasant shock when the actors emerge from the wings or trickle out of the darkened setting, called by our applause, and stand before us unmasked, as themselves, villain and hero hand in hand. The stage is suddenly a stage, the costume a costume (work clothes), the actor's bow a modest admission of virtuosity; *Hamlet* was, finally, insubstantial—a text, no more, on which one might practice this art of transcendental hypocrisy.

Index